Nana's Italian Cookies

and other Biscotto Recipes from Italy

Copyright © 2020, 2021,2022   Virginia N. Pipitone, White Wolf Unlimited, LLC.
First published December 2020. 2nd Edition October 2022. ISBN: 979-8-9850960-0-2

Visit our store online: **CookiesAroundTheWorld.com**

For information, contact author at: vnpipitone@whitewolfunlimited.us

White Wolf Unlimited, LLC. 12470 York Street, #52, East Lake, Colorado, USA 80614

To the best of the author's knowledge, all information contained herein is true,
accurate, and complete. Recipe ingredients and directions are made without guarantee
on the part of the author/publisher, and disclaim any liability in connection with the use
of this information.

Nana's Italian Cookies

and other Biscotto Recipes from Italy

Virginia N. Pipitone

Healing the World one Cookie at a time!

Cookies Around the World

Mission & Vision

Our **Mission** is to promote cultural awareness
around the world through international cookie recipes books.

Our **Vision** is to help in the fight against world hunger,
especially as it impacts children.

A portion of all proceeds from the sale of this book
and other items sold through our website
is donated to agencies striving to end world hunger.

You can help by shopping for any Amazon purchase
using our website: ***www.CookiesAroundTheWorld.com***

Grazzi,

Virginia N. Pipitone

Healing the World one Cookie at a time!

Dedication

My Sicilian mother-in-law, Mary Russo Pipitone — "Nana — cooked wonderful Italian meals. Still, we would tease her any way that her red sauce needed more practice just so she would make it again. Her sauces were superb, but it was at the oven baking where she was indeed in her glory. Months before Christmas, she would begin baking cookies, cookies, and more cookies! Soon, her freezer would overflow in anticipation of the holiday season.

Nana grew up in Rochester, New York. She married Joseph Pipitone, a hardworking Italian of Neapolitan descent, and raised two children. Mary and Joe's children escaped the Rochester winters and moved to Florida. After Joe retired, he and Nana followed their children south. They became "Florida Snowbirds," wintering in the Sunshine State and driving back to their small retirement cottage on Lake Ontario for the summer.

With grandparents nearby for the holidays, the growing family of kids, grandkids, and even great-grands always looked forward to Nana's Christmas cookies. It would not feel like the holidays without them. Each family member had his or her favorites: Pizzelles, Almond Cherry Macaroons, Pineapple Stars, Slivered Almond, Chocolate Spice, Venetian Torts, and Wandies. I remember the year I convinced her to teach me her recipes — we baked cookies all weekend! She even gave me some of her small metal sheets, custom-made by her brother, Luis Russo, which she used when icing the Venetian Torts with chocolate.

Sadly, Nana passed away unexpectedly in 2006 at 84 years old, the same year my Italian husband and I divorced. Despite no longer being a part of the immediate family, I have kept her cherished handwritten recipes all these years. I am excited to showcase them in this cookbook and other fine cookie recipes direct from Italy and local Italian-Americans. Mary was not the only cook and baker in her family. Her brothers were equally talented. Like most Italians I know, they showed their love by cooking and baking for their families. It was ample excuse for fun-filled family gatherings — often all-day events. I still miss those happy gatherings. The Italians sure know how to enjoy life!

I hope this book honors Mary and all Italian grandmothers. May it inspire you to have your own Italian gathering full of fun, love, and delicious cookies!

Dedicated to the memory of a truly wonderful Italian mother-in-law.

Mary Russo Pipitone
August 1, 1922 - October 6, 2006

Acknowledgements

Baking cookies brings the family together. With younger ones learning how to mix and measure, parents and grandparents passing on their recipes, and everyone getting creative with frosting and sprinkles, cookies are never really made alone.
Neither was this book.

Special thanks to Mary's daughter and granddaughter, Jeanie Pipitone Ortiz and Kristen A. Pipitone (*PipSqueaking* food and wine blogger), for their help tracking down and reviewing her recipes.

A heartfelt thanks to Mary's nephew, Louis Russo, Jr., who graciously provide other recipes handed down from his father, Louis Russo, Sr, and friends.

Thanks also to my editor, William Bostwick, for his inspirational writing and editing, and to my word processor, Myriam Parker, who was able to transcribe recipes for me.

My daughter and her husband (culinary chef), Danielle and Jamie Glass, for their input, research, and administrative support.

With much gratitude to John Lavenia and fellow members of the JL Success Mastermind group who consistently provided encouraging support during this endeavor, you are like family to me.

Grazie a tutti!

Virginia

Table of Contents

From Italy with Love

Italy is a world unto itself, with its own rules, customs, traditions, and, of course, cuisine. It's a world of subtlety and contrast, vibrant yet relaxed. Appointment times and traffic lights are merely suggestions. *Pasticcerias* advertise their fresh-baked delicacies with aromas wafting from their open doors. The tiniest thimble of espresso might last an entire afternoon at an outdoor café. At the same time, a bottle of vino might disappear before you know it.

If Italy is its own world, its twenty regions can seem like sovereign nations, with dialects, histories, and cultures all their own. This book draws from all of them —primarily Sicily, Southern Italy, Piedmont, Tuscany, and Venice. But the recipes here are not meant to be sacred talismans of some pure, authentic Italian culture. They reflect the Italian diaspora when home cooks had to adapt to new ingredients and new environments. This is genuinely Italian-American cuisine. It's complicated. Some of the cookies here have different names in different towns or regions. Some don't have English translations, and some don't have common Italian names at all. But trust me — they are all delicious.

I've done my best to accurately record each recipe and instruction. Of course, your results may vary, depending on the ingredients used, water chemistry, altitude, and the many other factors that affect what goes on in a kitchen. If you know of different names for these cookies, have insight into their history, or have any other contributions, please share in a review of this cookbook on Amazon or our Facebook page: @CookiesAroundTheWorld.

Thanks, and Buon Appetito!

Regions of Italy

History, Legend, and Folklore

Italian food is rich in more than flavor. Food looms large in Italian culture. Some might say that in Italy, food *is* culture. So, it's no surprise that every part of Italian cuisine has its own deep history, own stories, and own myths and legends. Take, for example, the humble almond. First introduced to Italy by Arab traders, they became associated with good fortune and are to this day still common gifts at weddings. In Sicily, the almond tree is a symbol of love — but the connection goes back even further, into ancient Greek mythology.

It is no surprise, then, that there seems to be an entire realm of influences for every kind of Italian cookie (biscotto) - some real historical roots, some simply folklore, or tradition. Indeed, small and delicate as they sometimes are, cookies might carry the most traditional weight of any piece of Italian cuisine. At weddings and funerals, on Christmas and Easter, on feast days, birthdays, or any old day of the week, cookies can be found. A meal is not complete without dessert — and Italian culture is not complete without cookies.

Of course, when we talk about Italian food, we're really talking about Italian-American food. This is especially true of cookies. Italian bakeries provided more than just bread to the waves of Italian immigrants flooding the US in the nineteenth and early twentieth century. They offered the comforts of home as well. One of these comforts was cookies. Every region in Italy has its own styles, shapes, and flavors, influenced by the fruits and nuts that grow best there. And every Italian family has its own book of cookie recipes, passed from nana (*nonna*) to granddaughter to great-granddaughter. At these bakeries, at the family dinner table, in every cookie jar, at every wedding banquet, cookies build community, connecting Italian-Americans of every generation to their home, to their past, and to each other.

Amaretti - Almond Cookies
Amaretti, which means "little bitter things," are traditionally made from both bitter and sweet almonds (or almond paste). Widely popular throughout Italy, the dome-shaped cookies vary slightly based on region. They may be chewy or crunchy, with a bit of vanilla or lemon zest. Some might substitute apricot kernels if bitter almonds are not available. Venetians claim they invented the cookie during the Renaissance. Others say it dates back to the Middle Ages in Arab-ruled Sicily.

Amaretti di Saronno remains crisp and dry; can be used as an ingredient in other Italian Desserts recipes. *Amaretti di Sassello* stays crunchy on the outside yet chewy and softer on the inside.

Anginetti - Lemon cookies

Many Italian-American families with roots in southern Italy know and expect these cookies at every family event. Since butter was not common in southern Italy, many recipes from that area use oil or shortening instead. Lemon is the typical flavoring, but orange and anise are frequently added.

Baci di Dama – Lady's Kisses

Literally translated as "lady's kisses," *Baci di Dama* were named, legend has it because the two cookies sandwiched together resemble a woman's lips. Light and delicate, they were made famous at the pastry shops of Tortona in the Piedmont region. Made from finely ground hazelnuts and nestled together with a dollop of dark, silky chocolate, these cookies are sweet as a kiss.

Biscotti - Twice-Baked Cookies

This popular Italian cookie traces its origins to Ancient Rome and was a staple food for humble travelers and the Roman Legion alike. *Biscotti* means "twice-baked." These hard cookies are baked as a long loaf, then sliced and baked a second time to completely dry the slices. This process results in a hard and dry texture but with a very long shelf life, making them both durable for travel and nutrient-rich for long journeys. Biscotti regained popularity during the Renaissance in Tuscany, where they were served with sweet wine for dunking. Initially flavored with almonds, they are now made in dozens of flavors.

Biscotti al Burro - Butter Cookies

The butter cookies in America bear little resemblance to those you will find in Italy. Still, they are an essential part of any Italian-American bakery in this country. Butter, sugar, and flour make for a simple, classic cookie. Use a mixture of both butter and shortening for a cookie that crumbles but is not too dry.

Biscotti all'Anice - Anise Cookies

Italians have used anise in cookies for hundreds of years. With their black licorice aroma, anise cookies are sweet little bites of heaven, usually distinguished by a light glaze.

Biscotti di San Valentino – St. Valentine cookies

The patron saint of love really existed, and he was Italian! Saint Valentine was born in Terni, a small town in central Umbria, sometime in the third century, and lived most of his life in Rome, where he married Christian couples secretly. When Emperor Claudius II demanded Valentino renounce his faith, he, of course, refused and was martyred on February 14, 269. For more than 200 years after his death,

Valentino was one of the many saints whose feast days were only lightly observed at Mass. However, in the fifth century, the Catholic Church decided to link his story with the ancient Roman fertility festival *Lupercalia*, celebrated from February 13 to 15, and Valentine's Day was born! Our Valentine's Day cookies are heart-shaped, of course, with rich, red filling.

Biscotti Regina – Queen's Biscuits
The *Biscotti Regina* or *Reginelle*, while originally from Palermo, are found all around Sicily. They taste halfway between sweet and savory, reminiscent of their roots in Arab cuisine, and are usually coated with sesame seeds.

Bocconotti - Small Bites
More of a pastry than a cookie, these seductive rustic morsels are typical of the Apulia, Abruzzo, and Calabria regions. Often eaten at Christmas, *Bocconotti*, or "small bites," are stuffed with sweet fillings that vary by region. *Bocconotti Montoriesi* turn autumn's harvest of Montepulciano grapes into an irresistible dark stuffing. The famous *Bocconotto di Castel Frentano*, which originated towards the end of the 1700s, features chocolate and cinnamon as its filling.

Brutti ma Buoni - Ugly but Good
Also known as *Bruttiboni* and *Mandorlati di San Clemente*, these unevenly shaped almond or hazelnut cookies made with cooked meringue and chopped hazelnuts are fittingly named "ugly but good." Popular in Prato, in central Italy, these chewy, nutty cookies were created in 1878 by Constantino Veniani, in his pasticceria in Gavirote, a small town outside Milan. Their rich flavor of toasted hazelnuts coated in a crunchy meringue makes them truly irresistible.

Canestrelli - Little Baskets
These simple "little baskets," also called "egg yolk" cookies, have been around since the Middle Ages. Often used as gifts on festive occasions, they are made all over Italy but commonly associated with northern regions, especially Liguria. The most recognized variety is a pale, flower-shaped cookie with a hole in the center. They have a delicious, lemony flavor and are super-soft, with a light, crunchy bite. According to folklore, they were placed in baskets to dry, hence their name.

Cannoli Siciliani - Cannoli
Originating in Palermo, Sicily, and known world-wide *Cannoli*, the traditional forms of these cookies are tube-shaped pastry shells deep-fried and filled with creamy ricotta. Created for Carnevale season, *Pizzelles* can be used in place of the fried pastry shells, resulting in a lighter, less fatty version.

Chiacchiere di Carnevale - Carnevale Fritters
Carnevale, like Mardi Gras in the US, is celebrated in Italy, with costume parties and elaborate parades leading up to the solemn 40-days of Lent. These fried sweets are available in bakeries all over Italy during the Carnevale period. Cookie shapes

and textures range from flat, crispy ribbons and bow ties to puffy doughnuts. They are often dusted with confectioners' sugar or drizzled with honey. Common types are *Bugie, Castagnole, Cenci, Chiacchiere, Frappe, Guanti, Tortelli,* and *Zeppole.*

Ciambelle al Vino - Wine Cookies
Need a way to use leftover wine? Wine cookies are a perfect solution. A delicious, crunchy, but not too sweet cookie, popular in the fall, wine cookies fall apart in your mouth. Said to have originated in Naples, I'm not sure who created this cookie, but I like the way they think.

Cuccidati – Sicilian Fig Cookies
Traditional Christmas cookies originating from Sicilian bakers, adept at blending European and Arab baking traditions. Also known as *Buccellati*, the cookies come in many versions but are united by a special fig filling: a fragrant mix of dried figs, nuts, chocolate, candied fruit, and cinnamon. This rich fig jam is rolled into a moist, shortbread cookie shell. Shaped as a log or wreath, they remain fresh for a long time. *Cuccidati* is a very nostalgic cookie for many Sicilian-Americans.

Krumiri - Crooked Moustache
These cornmeal cookies from Casale Monferrato in Piedmont were created in 1878, the year of King Vittorio Emanuele II's death. The story goes that, after a night of revelry at a café, confectioner Domenico Rossi led his friends back to his kitchen for a late-night snack. There he invented what would become Piedmont's most famous cookie. Folklore has two possible reasons for the name. One holds that Rossi named his cookie after a liqueur called Krumiro, in honor of that late night out with his friends. The second possibility reflects Casale Monferrato's Jewish roots. The Yiddish word *krumm* means "crooked," just like the king's handlebar mustache!

Lingua di Gato – Cat's Tongue
Named after their characteristic oval shape and slightly rough texture (like a cat's tongue), these cookies are light, thin, and crunchy. They are best served with coffee or alongside ice cream desserts.

Mandorle Amaretti - Macaroons
The earliest recorded macaroon recipes are similar to an almond meringue, with a crisp crust and a soft interior. Historians claim that macaroons can be traced back to an Italian monastery in the ninth century.

Matrimonios – Wedding Cookies
Known by many different names around the globe, these cookies first appeared in Medieval Arab cuisine. Food historians speculate that the Moors brought them to Spain, from where the recipe quickly spread throughout Europe. This explains why wedding cookies from so many countries and cultures are so similar. No matter what, every wedding seems to have a similar type: a crumbly, shortbread dough made of sugar, flour, butter, and nuts, and rolled in confectioners' sugar.

Mostaccioli – Citrus Spice Cookies
The origin of this cookie is said to date back almost 2,500 years. When sugar was not readily available in ancient Italy, these cookies were sweetened with the pressed grapes leftover from making wine. They were made in different shapes and sizes with intricate patterns depicting animals, baskets, or palm trees and often sold at auctions to raise money for charities.

Muzetta - Chocolate Spice Balls
Traditional chocolate Christmas cookies, sometimes called "meatballs," are flavored with cinnamon and cloves and covered in a chocolate glaze. While they seem present at every Italian-American Christmas party, their origin is unknown.

Occhi di Bue – Bull's Eye
Often the most gigantic cookies in any Italian pastry shop. Despite their size, their construction is simple: a basic, sandwich-style cookie, cut into a generous, round shape with a thin layer of fruit preserves, fruit curd, or Nutella spread in between. The top half of every cookie has a smaller circle cut out, so the filling is visible.

Ossi dei Morti – Bones of the Dead
The name of these crunchy biscuits literally translates to "bones of the dead," referring to their visual appearance. They are traditionally prepared across the country on November 1st, All Saints Day, and served on November 2nd, All Souls Day, to honor and commemorate loved ones who have passed away. The key ingredient in this seasonal recipe is almond meal from almonds harvested in autumn. However, some regions use hazelnuts instead. When they are not paired with coffee or tea, *Ossi dei Morti* is best enjoyed with a glass of dessert wine.

Pasti di Mandorle – Sicilian Almond Cookies
Almonds are the primary ingredient of *Pasti di Mandorle*, a traditional Sicilian soft cookie. Unlike the Amaretti, these almond cookies do not use bitter almonds or apricot kernels. Instead, they can be flavored with lemon or orange zest, pistachio paste, coffee, or even chopped chocolate.

Pignoli - Pine Nut Cookies
"Pine nut" cookies are crispy on the outside, chewy on the inside, and rich in flavor and texture. Sometimes made with ground pine nuts in the batter but always rolled in pine nuts before baking. Wildly popular in southern Italy and Sicily.

Pizzelles
Pizzelle comes from the word *pizze*, which means flat and round. Pizzelles were initially made in Ortona, in the Abruzzo region of south-central Italy, around the eighth century. It is one of the oldest cookies and is believed to have developed from the ancient Roman baked good *crustulum*. The batter is poured between two plates of snowflake-patterned iron and held over a fire or heated electrically. Centuries ago, families had pizzelle irons made with family crests, special dates,

or celebratory designs. *Pizzelles* are almost always found at Italian weddings and religious celebrations. Anise is the traditional flavor, but modern versions include vanilla, peppermint, anisette, lemon, chocolate, and other flavor combinations.

Ricciarelli di Siena - Chewy Almond Cookies
Soft almond cookies dating back to the fourteenth century with attractive cracked tops and a pleasantly chewy texture. According to Sienese legend, they are named after a nobleman, Ricciardetto Della Gherardesca, who brought similar Arab sweets to Siena upon returning from the Crusades.

Salame di Cioccolato - Chocolate Salami
This is an intriguing little dessert that Italian families enjoy during lazy winter days with a cup of espresso. Named for its resemblance to salami, it is actually dark chocolate whisked with eggs and sugar to form a kind of mousse and thickened with crumbled tea biscuits. An uncooked cookie is an added advantage to this quick and easy recipe but remember to keep it refrigerated.

Savoiardi - Lady Fingers
Named after the House of Savory, Italy's last monarchs, Lady Fingers are a simple cookie with a very long history, dating all the way back to the 1300s. Originally from Piedmont, *Savoiardi* spread to other areas where the Savoys ruled, including Sardinia and Sicily. In Sardinia, they are flat; in Sicily, they are usually oval; in other cities, they are round. Regardless, this is, basically, a sponge cake that is dried out a bit during baking. As such, they soak up flavors easily and are often used in dessert recipes like *Tiramsu*.

Taralli Dolci di Pasque - Easter Ring Cookies
From the Puglia region of Southern Italy, these large, round cookies are traditionally made for Easter. Sometimes called Easter "rings", they are lightly sweet vanilla cookies coated with citrus icing. At other times of the year, *Taralli* can take on a savory flavor, with ingredients like black pepper, fennel, white wine.

Tricolore - Italian Flag, Venetian Torts
This cookie represents the Italian flag and is often referred to by Italians as *il Tricolore*. This cookie is made with three equally-sized layers of green, white, and red almond-based cake with preserves between the layers. Also known as Napoleons, Rainbow cookies, or Seven-layer cookies, my mother-in-law always called them Venetian Torts.

Zaletti - Polenta Cookies
When wheat became very expensive in the Middle Ages, bakers started incorporating cornmeal or polenta into their recipes. These rustic cookies acquired their name from the word *zálo*, which means "yellow" in the Venetian dialect. An easy recipe usually flavored with lemon zest; they are extra yummy with rum-soaked raisins. Traditionally made without sugar, a splash of grappa is often added to the dough.

The Wedding?
I'm here for
the Cookies

When you attend a traditional Italian wedding reception, be prepared for great food and even better desserts. An Italian reception usually includes a dessert table laden with the customary, white-tiered wedding cake, delicious desserts symbolizing luck and prosperity, and, of course, the Biscotti Cake.

Thought to have originated in Sicily and popular among many Italian-Americans, the Biscotti Cake, or Cookie Cake, is a substantial layered tower of traditional Italian cookies, decorated with candies and ribbons and flowers. These delicious cookies are often the result of the tremendous love and hard work of the mothers, grandmothers, relatives, and dear friends of the bride and groom, who spent countless hours in the kitchen preparing for the big event.

Shortly after the guests have finished dinner, the traditional white wedding cake is served with coffee and liqueurs. This allows the newlyweds time to visit guest tables and hand out confetti (candy-coated almonds) - a symbol that they will face life's bitter and sweet moments together in their marriage. (It also provides a discreet way to accept gift envelopes from generous guests!)

The Cookie Cake remains on display during the reception and is usually served toward the latter part of the evening. Traditionally, the bride and groom lead a chain of guests in a wedding march as the orchestra plays the Tarantella, an Italian folk song. They dance around the room, forming a circle, and march to the Cookie Cake to grab a treat as they dance by. After the train has passed, the non-dancing guests are allowed a cookie or two. Many Italian-Americans feel a reception is not complete without the Cookie Cake.

In fact, the Cookie Cake is so popular in some communities, do not be surprised if you see it at birthdays, anniversaries, religious events, and even funeral gatherings. It is often a chance for proud bakers to show off their best work!

Cookie cakes are held together with a light icing, which keeps its many layers from falling apart, mainly when it is being transported — and picked at by hungry guests! I didn't know this trick before my wedding, so I asked my Italian mother-in-law, what keeps the Cookie Cake from falling over. My father-in-law replied, "we use cement!"

Lieber, Ron (2009, December 15). The Wedding? I'm Here for the Cookies. *The New York Times.* https://www.nytimes.com/2009/12/16/dining/16cookies.html   Retrieved 10/21/20

Esposito, M. A., & dePaola, T. (1995). *Celebrations, Italian Style: Recipes and Menus for Special Occasions and Seasons of the Year* (1st ed.). Hearst Books.

Italian Wedding Cake photo. Jason Winkeler Photography, St. Louis, MO

Common Baking Ingredients

When baking, always use the freshest and best ingredients you can get. Butter left in the fridge too long can pick up odors. Old eggs will not rise as well as fresh eggs. Baking powder can lose its effectiveness after just six months. Nuts and spices can get rancid and lose their aroma. With quality ingredients and a little know-how, you will taste the difference in your cookies. Here are some essential tips, tricks, and information for the most common baking ingredients.

<u>Dairy</u>

- **Butter, unsalted**: Most bakers agree that unsalted butter is the default choice unless your recipe specifies otherwise. Butter gives baked goods a rich flavor and texture, with a luscious taste that simply cannot be replicated. Butter can be frozen until you need it. Cold butter works best for icings and when creaming with sugar.
- **Eggs**: Eggs help bind ingredients together. Select large eggs (white or brown) for most recipes. Always keep eggs refrigerated.
- **Milk**: Milk gives batters their moisture. Whole milk gives the richest flavor, but you can substitute low-fat milk to reduce fat content.
- **Buttermilk**: Buttermilk reacts with leaveners to make fluffier baked goods.
- **Alternative kinds of milk**: Can be made from soy, rice, coconut, or nuts. Since they are not as rich, your finished results may vary.
- **Evaporated milk**: This thick, concentrated dairy product doesn't require refrigeration and can be added to custards, pie fillings, and more for some extra thickness and creaminess.
- **Cream cheese**: Used in cookie batters and other baked goods, it also makes creamy frostings.
- **Ricotta cheese**: The production of ricotta cheese in the Italian peninsula dates back to the Bronze Age. Mild in taste with creamy white curds, ricotta cheese

- is a good ingredient for adding texture. Made from the milk of sheep, cows, goats, and even Italian water buffalo.

<u>Fats</u>

- **Butter**: See Dairy above.
- **Margarine**: Margarine is made from vegetable oil. Many of the recipes included call for margarine. This is probably because it was popular when our Nana raised her kids — it was cheap and yielded good results.
- **Shortening**: This is a solid vegetable fat used by some cooks to replace butter or, in combination with butter, to make tender baked goods like pie crusts. Shortening has a higher melting point than butter, so cookies made with shortening tend to keep their shape better.
- **Vegetable oils**: Vegetable oil has a neutral flavor and is useful in recipes and deep-frying. Canola oil, which is a slightly healthier vegetable oil made from rapeseed, is preferred.
- **Olive oil**: Olive oil is a staple of Italian cuisine with a distinct flavor. Some traditional Italian cookies, like biscotti, are made with olive oil. It imparts a fruity flavor and goes well with baked goods containing citrus, chocolate, or nuts—select cold-pressed Extra Virgin Olive Oil.

Butter vs. Margarine

Butter-based cookies are crispier, with sturdy edges, a distinct chew, and a richer flavor. Butter's high-fat content gives baked goods their texture. Margarine results in tender chewiness but does not have the flavor of butter. You can add butter extract to compensate. Margarine, which can contain more water and less fat, may make thin cookies spread while baking and may burn. Some bakers like to use a mixture of half butter and half margarine.

Butter vs. Shortening

Butter and shortening can substitute in equal amounts. Since butter melts at a lower temperature, cookies may spread more and bake flatter than when made with shortening. Butter results in crispier cookies if there is a significant amount of sugar in the recipe. If using all butter, try chilling the dough first to help reduce its spread when baking. Again, consider using a mix of half butter and half shortening.

Flour

- **All-purpose flour:** AP flour is the go-to flour for most baking. Made from a blend of high-gluten hard wheat and low-gluten soft wheat, its light and fluffy texture comes from being milled to remove all wheat germ and bran. Use an unbleached variety unless you have specific dietary restrictions. If so, you might try using whole wheat all-purpose flour, gluten-free, rye, or buckwheat flours. Keep in mind, you will need to make recipe adjustments when using a different flour. *Farina 00* is Italy's all-purpose flour. Graded by the extraction rate (how much bran and germ have been removed), it is the most highly refined flour. It feels silky to the touch, never sandy or gritty.
- **Alternate non-wheat flours**: Flour milled from other grains, nuts, or seeds.
- **Bread flour**: Bread flour contains more protein and more gluten. It is ideal for baking chewy yeasted bread.
- **Cake flour**: This flour is lower in protein and gluten than all-purpose flour. It is chemically treated and finely ground to produce cakes with a lighter texture.
- **Cornmeal (Polenta):** Polenta is a coarse ground flour made from dry corn and used in place of flour in some desserts. Its slightly gritty, sandy texture results in crispier baked goods. In the past, polenta was commonly used by the poor who could not afford wheat flour.
- **Cornstarch**: Finely ground corn flour used for thickening sauces and fillings.
- **Pastry flour**: Made from low-protein wheat, pastry flour is low in gluten, resulting in light, fluffy pastries.
- **Self-Rising flour**: All-purpose flour with baking powder and salt already mixed in.
- **Whole-grain flour**: Whole-grain flour retains the entire kernel of the grain.
- **Whole-wheat flour**: This flour contains the germ and is often used to replace a portion of all-purpose flour in a recipe to boost its nutritional profile.

How to store flours

Generally, you can store flour in airtight, moisture-proof containers on a cool, dark shelf or in the refrigerator. Some flours spoil quicker than others, such as whole-wheat and whole-grain flours, because they contain more grain elements. To extend shelf life, store these flours in the refrigerator or freezer. Alternative flours often contain more plant oils and should be stored in the fridge or freezer after opening. It is always best to read and follow the manufacturer's recommendations for safe storage.

Leaveners

To create light, airy baked goods, it's necessary to add a leavening agent. Leaveners cause chemical reactions, filling batters and dough with tiny gas bubbles that help baked goods rise, either in the mixing process or when heated.

- **Baking soda**: Baking soda's acid component reacts with heat to make baked goods rise.
- **Baking powder**: Made of baking soda, powdered acid, and cornstarch. Double-acting means the baking powder forms carbon dioxide bubbles when mixed into batter or dough and again when heated.
- **Yeast**: Considered a biological, slow-rising agent because it takes time for yeast cells to naturally metabolize and create carbon dioxide.

Baking soda vs. Baking powder
If you think baking soda and baking powder are interchangeable, think again. Baking powder already contains baking soda, cornstarch, and a powdered acid, so no additional ingredients are needed to activate the leavening process. Baking soda must be combined with an acidic ingredient, such as vinegar, citrus juice, cream of tartar, cocoa powder, or fermented dairies like yogurt or buttermilk.

Salt

- **Granulated table salt**: Salt used for everyday baking. Some bakers prefer to use un-iodized table salt because they can detect an unpleasant flavor from iodized salt.
- **Kosher salt**: A coarse-grained, non-iodized salt made from salt crystals; may contain an anti-caking agent. The evaporation process determines the shape, so kosher salt can be flat or pyramidal.
- **Sea salt**: Salt harvested from evaporated seawater. Crunchy and flaky, it's often sprinkled across sweet baked goods to add texture and flavor.

Sugar

- **Granulated sugar**: The most commonly used sugar in recipes. It is made from sugarcane or beets juice, stripped of natural molasses, then refined again, resulting in white sugar. Raw sugar, however, retains its tan color.
- **Confectioners' sugar (powdered sugar)**: These are the same thing with different names and sometimes labeled as 10X. Made from granulated sugar that has been ground into ultra-fine particles and mixed with a small amount of cornstarch to prevent caking. Dissolving quickly in liquid, these are the gold standards for glazes and frostings. Many cookies are rolled in or dusted with these sugars for a finishing touch and added sweetness.
- **Brown sugar**: Brown sugar is a combination of white granulated sugar and molasses, resulting in a moist, slightly sticky texture and darker color. The amount of molasses in the mix accounts for a range of colors and flavors from light to dark brown sugars. They can be used interchangeably, but dark brown sugar has a more significant impact on taste. When measuring out brown sugar, press it down firmly into the measuring cup or spoon until it is fully compacted and level.
- **Superfine sugar (castor sugar)**: Castor sugar is ground into tiny crystals that dissolve very quickly. Great for making meringues and sweetening whipped cream. It can be substituted for regular granulated sugar one-to-one. Fine-grained sugars like this blend easier with butter and dough.
- **Sanding sugar (decorating or coarse sugar)**: Sanding sugar merely is larger crystals of granulated sugar and gives baked goods a crystalline finish. It is available in many different colors.
- **Corn syrup**: Adding both sweetness and moisture to a recipe, corn syrup is sometimes used as an alternative to granulated sugar.
- **Other natural sugars**: Date sugar, coconut sugar, maple sugar, honey, molasses, maple syrup, cane syrup, and agave nectar are some examples. All add a different flavor of sweetness.

Extra Ingredients

Chocolate

Italians in the Piedmont region have been making *cioccolato* from cocoa beans and sugar since the sixth century. The percentage of cacao tells what portion of the chocolate comes from cocoa beans. The higher the number, the more intense the chocolate taste, and the less sweet it is.

- **Milk chocolate**: Made with milk or milk powder, this sweet chocolate is the lightest in color.
- **Dark chocolate**: Bittersweet and semisweet chocolates are interchangeable when baking. Similar in taste and composition, you can substitute either in equal amounts. Bittersweet chocolate squares work best in most recipes because they melt quicker than semisweet chocolate chips. Three tablespoons of chocolate chips equal one ounce of baking chocolate.
- **Unsweetened chocolate**: Unsweetened chocolate may be substituted for bittersweet chocolate. Combine 2/3-ounce unsweetened chocolate with 2 teaspoons of sugar for each ounce of bittersweet chocolate.
- **Cocoa powder**: Cocoa powder is what remains after cocoa butter is extracted from the beans, leaving behind just the bitter solids. Available as natural, with a slightly acidic flavor, and Dutch-processed (alkalized) with a less acidic and milder flavor. To use as a substitute for bittersweet chocolate, add one tablespoon of cocoa powder, one tablespoon of sugar, and two teaspoons of butter to your recipe for each ounce of bittersweet chocolate needed.
- **White chocolate**: Chocolate made of cocoa, butter, milk, and sugar, without the chocolate solids, resulting in a white color.

Dried Fruit

Dried fruits have a long tradition of use, dating back to the fourth millennium BC in Mesopotamia. They are prized for their sweet taste, nutritional value, and long shelf life. In baked goods, they boost texture and moisture levels. High in fiber and carbohydrates but low in fat, these shrunken versions of their fresh counterparts are very dense in calories.

- **Apricots**: Many varieties are available but look for those that are soft and fresh. If they are slightly hard, warm them in a little water or other liquid to soften before chopping.
- **Coconut**: Can come shredded or flaked, sweetened or unsweetened. For macaroons, use unsweetened coconut. Cookies made with unsweetened coconut will not be as sweet but will be crispier.
- **Cranberries**: Known for their tangy taste and potential health benefits (high in vitamin C), dried cranberries are often sweetened with glycerin or oil and sugar to make them palatable.
- **Dates**: Extremely sweet, and extremely nutrient-dense, dried dates undergo an intensive dehydration process giving them a very long shelf life of one year or longer.
- **Figs**: High in fiber and rich in iron, figs are used widely in Italian baked goods. The two most common varieties are Black Mission and Calimyrna.
- **Raisins**: These are the most popular dried fruits. Usually made from Thompson grapes, dark raisins are the most common, but golden raisins are also available. Currant raisins are made from the Black Corinth grape; tiny, seedless, and very sweet.

To enjoy dried fruits at their best:
Store the fruit in a cool, dark, dry place, and use within six months. Once opened, it is best to close the bag and store the fruit in the refrigerator to slow oxidation and keep it from drying out.

Extracts and Flavorings:

Flavor isn't just an additive; it's the absolute essence of baking. Extracts and flavorings tempt the palate and delight the senses without affecting the structure of your baked goods. You can substitute one for another in equal parts or increase or decrease the amount in a recipe to meet your flavor preferences. *Extracts* usually are alcohol-based and very concentrated with intense flavors. A little goes a long way!
Flavorings are water- or oil-based and are not chemical imitations.

- **Almond**: With a robust, nutty, yet sweet flavor, almond extract is second only to vanilla in popularity.
- **Anise:** Anise is the traditional flavor in various Italian baked goods, such as pizzelles and aniseed cookies. It has a flavor similar to licorice or fennel.
- **Butter**: Use this to enhance or impart a butter flavor in recipes using margarine or shortening.
- **Citrus**: Orange, lemon, and lime, among others, add a freshness to recipes.
- **Fiori di Sicilia**: The Flower of Sicily is floral with orange notes. In the US, most Fiori di Sicilia extracts are combinations of vanilla and orange extract.
- **Liquor**: Use to impart a liquor flavor without the actual alcohol. Brandy and rum are popular choices.
- **Pure Vanilla**: Gives baked goods a warm, spicy aroma and flavor. It is available both as a liquid and a paste. Vanilla extract is made from soaking real vanilla beans in alcohol and water.

Food Coloring

A dye or pigment additive that imparts color when added to dough, icings, and sugars. Found in most grocery stores' baking area, usually in red, yellow, blue, and green. Mix them to make a rainbow of colors and shades. Available in liquid, gels, powders, and pastes.

Liquor & Liqueurs

Alcohol, either distilled and aged liquors or sweetened or flavored liqueurs, isn't just an after-dinner treat — it can play a role in the kitchen as well. Liquor and liqueurs add lots of flavor and moisture to baked goods.

- **Anisette (Anis)**: An anise-flavored liqueur that is consumed in most Mediterranean countries. Containing sugar, it is colorless and sweeter than dry anise-flavored liqueurs.
- **Brandy**: Liquor produced by distilling wine. Brandy generally contains 35-60% alcohol by volume (70-120 proof) and is typically consumed as an after-dinner digestif. The term "brandy" also denotes liquors obtained from the distillation of pomace, mash, or wine of any other fruit. Also known as *eau de vie* or "water of life," fruit-flavored brandies are typically very light.
- **Grappa**: Grappa is one of Italy's most popular alcoholic drinks. A fragrant, grape-based pomace brandy, it can only be called "grappa" if it's sourced and produced in Italy. Made from pomace (the pressed grape skins and seeds left over from wine production), grappa contains 35-60% alcohol by volume. Clear and colorless, it is distilled for smoothness and clarity. High-quality versions are produced from the pomace of Italy's best-known grapes, which impart their aromatic flavors. In Italy, grappa is served very cold as an after-dinner drink to aid digestion and is also used in baking and cooking recipes.

Nuts (*Noci*):

Choose whole nuts with even color. Nuts have lots of oil and can go rancid quickly, so it is best to store them in the freezer until you are ready to bake.

- **Almonds (*Mandorle*):** Grown widely in Sicily, almonds are symbols of good fortune. Almonds can be bought raw with skins on, blanched and peeled, slivered, or flaked. Also available as a paste, butter, or ground flour. 1½ cups of almond paste equal 1 pound of almonds.
- **Hazelnuts (*Nocciole*):** Grown in several regions of Italy, hazelnuts originated from the Piedmont region. The skins can be removed by toasting then rubbing together vigorously in a clean, flat-weave dish towel.
- **Walnuts (*Noce*):** Grown in Italy's central regions, recipes calling for walnuts go back many centuries. Probably the first nut cultivated in Italy, and history credits the Romans with introducing the tree to England.
- **Pine nuts (*Pinoli*):** Harvesting these small nuts from pine cones takes a lot of labor, which is why they are expensive. Used sparingly, usually on the outside of cookies.
- **Pistachios (*Pistacchi*):** Sicily is a major producer of green elongated, narrow pistachios. Grown in the rich volcanic soil surrounding Mount Etna, Sicily, Sicilian pistachios are highly prized for their verdant green color and pronounced flavor,

How to toast nuts:

Toasting brings out even more of a nut's flavor. Spread nuts on a baking sheet or jelly roll pan in a single layer and Bake at 350°F (180°C) for 10-15 minutes, shaking the pan occasionally or turning them with a metal spatula. You'll smell their aroma as they are toasting. Immediately move them to a clean bowl to cool before grinding them or using them in recipes. Toasted nuts can be stored in the fridge or freezer to extend their shelf life.

Preserves, Jams, and Jellies:

Sweet fruit preserves are mostly used as condiments or spreads or as ingredients in pastries or desserts. There is a distinct difference between the types, and using the wrong one when baking can significantly alter your results.

- **Preserves**: Cooked and gelled whole fruit that includes a significant portion of the fruit.
- **Jam**: In jams, the fruit is cut into pieces or crushed, then heated with water and sugar until it gels.
- **Jelly**: Clear, sparkling with a fresh fruit flavor, jelly is processed similar to making jam but with extra liquid added and the fruit pulp filtered out. Jelly should quiver slightly when moved but hold angles when cut.

Spices

Ever since Marco Polo brought exotic spices back to Venice from the Far East, Italians have loved using them in their recipes. Spices are the dried seeds, bark, fruit, or roots of a plant. To intensify their flavor, toast spices briefly before grinding.

- **Allspice**: A dried, unripe berry from a mid-canopy tree. The name "allspice" was used as early as 1621 by the English, who valued it as a spice with the flavors of cinnamon, nutmeg, and clove.
- **Anise or aniseed**: The seed from a flowering plant native to the Mediterranean. Its flavor and aroma are very similar to star anise, fennel, and licorice.
- **Cinnamon**: As early as 2000 BC, cinnamon was used not only for flavor but even by the Egyptians to embalm mummies! Taken from the cinnamon tree's inner bark, it is the most commonly used spice in baking due to its warm and cozy aromatic flavor.
- **Cloves**: The aromatic flower buds of a tree native to Indonesia, this pungent spice is used in savory dishes, desserts, and drinks. Often combined in sweet desserts with cinnamon and nutmeg.
- **Nutmeg**: To get that warm, slightly sweet flavor and aromatic fragrance, buy whole nutmeg seeds, then grate the amount you need fresh for the recipe.
- **Sesame seeds:** Domesticated well over 3,000 years ago, sesame has one of the highest oil contents of any seed. With a rich, nutty flavor, it is a common ingredient in cuisines across the world. Like other seeds, it can trigger allergic reactions in some people.

How to buy spices:

The best way to buy your spices is in bulk, buying only a little at a time, so they do not get stale and loose flavor. All the recipes here use ground spices unless otherwise indicated. Pre-ground spices are convenient, but to get the absolute freshest taste, grind your own! This is quickly done with a microplane or old-fashioned mortar and pestle.

Sprinkles

These very tiny candies are produced in various shapes and colors. They are generally used as a topping or a decorative element.

Caution - Food Allergies

Many of the recipes have ingredients that are considered common food allergens and may cause an allergic reaction. Please use caution when serving guests, especially children. The following is extracted from KidsHealth.org.

Common foods (in baked goods) that may trigger a reaction are:
- Milk
- Eggs
- Wheat
- Tree nuts (e.g., almonds, walnuts, pecans)
- Peanuts
- Raw fruit & nuts
- Sesame seeds

Food allergy reactions can vary from person to person. Sometimes the same person can react differently at different times. It is crucial to quickly identify and treat food allergy reactions.

Reactions can:
- be very mild and only involve one part of the body, like hives on the skin
- be more severe and affect more than one part of the body
- happen within a few minutes or up to two hours after contact with the food

Food allergy reactions can affect any of these four areas of the body:

1. **skin**: itchy red bumps (hives); eczema; redness and swelling of the face or extremities; itching and swelling of the lips, tongue, or mouth (skin reactions are the most common type of reaction)

2. **gastrointestinal tract**: belly pain, nausea, vomiting, or diarrhea

3. **respiratory system**: runny or stuffy nose, sneezing, coughing, wheezing, shortness of breath

4. **cardiovascular system**: lightheadedness or fainting

Sometimes, an allergy can cause a severe anaphylaxis reaction, even if a previous reaction was mild. Anaphylaxis might start with some of the same symptoms as a less severe reaction but can quickly get worse. The person may have trouble breathing or pass out. More than one part of the body might be involved. If it is not treated, anaphylaxis can be life-threatening. **Seek immediate medical attention.**

Kids Health from Nemours. https://kidshealth.org/en/parents/food-allergies.html. Retrieved 10/27/20

Baking Utensils, Tools, and Equipment

Even if you have never baked before, you can tackle any project with a good recipe and the right equipment. This may seem like a long list, but don't worry — you certainly don't need every piece of equipment here. There are plenty you probably already own, hidden in the back of a cabinet or bottom drawer. Use what you have, and upgrade when you can.

Aluminum foil: Aluminum foil is used for many baking needs. You can transform a dark baking sheet into a lighter one by covering it with aluminum foil — just make sure to grease the foil to keep your cookies from sticking.

Beaters: Stand and hand-held mixers usually come with several attachments. A stand mixer will often have a balloon whisk attachment. In contrast, a hand-held mixer is typically equipped with a pair of sturdy, stainless-steel beaters.

Bench scraper: A metal bench scraper is the baking world's chef's knife: indispensable and used for just about everything. You'll use a scraper to mix and fold soft dough, cut through plump dough, and scrape sticky dough loose from the counter. A scraper with a reasonably sharp edge and comfortable handle across the top edge is best. Some even come stamped with rulers on the bottom, which are handy for measuring cookie ropes and logs.

Brushes: Pastry brushes are convenient for applying egg wash to doughs for a shiny finish.

Cookie baking sheets: These come in many materials, thicknesses, and finishes, with rims and without. Their shapes vary from flat pans for cookies to shaped tins for molded desserts. Thick sheets with a light finish are best for cookies. Aluminum sheets transfer heat better than steel sheets. Avoid dark, nonstick sheets for their tendency to over-brown the bottoms of cookies.

Cookie cutters: Available in metal and hard plastic, cookie cutters come in all shapes and sizes. Widely popular to make Christmas and Easter cookies, they have thin, sharp cutting edges and rounded or rubber-coated tops. Make sure your cutters are at least 1 inch high to cut through thick dough.

Cookie press: A long cylinder with a plunger on one end and a metal die-cut disc at the other, cookie presses squeeze cookie dough into perfect shapes directly onto your baking sheet. They can be fitted with many kinds of shaped disks, such as stars, flowers, fleur-de-lis, leaves, shells, wreaths, pinwheels, and snowflakes.

Dry measuring cups: Used for measuring dry ingredients. Choose heavy, well-constructed, stainless-steel cups with markings that are easy to read even when the cup is full. Markings on the handles are most practical.

Food processor: Most food processors can make quick work of grinding nuts into meal or flour, but to make a dough, you will need a strong motor and a work bowl with a capacity of at least 11-14 cups. Look for one with a large, oval feed tube and heavy, stable base.

Hand-held mixer: A hand-held mixer will perform all the same baking tasks (except kneading dough) as a more expensive stand mixer, so it's a good option for budget- or space-conscious bakers. The mixer should be comfortable to hold and easy to maneuver around a bowl. A simple, slim beater without a central post is best so that batter does not collect around the post.

Liquid measuring cups: A simple Pyrex cup with red lines and a pour spout is the industry standard. It is easy to use, accurate, and durable. Glass cups will retain their measuring lines better than plastic ones.

Measuring spoons: Use heavy, well-constructed, stainless-steel models with long, sturdy, well-designed handles. They should have flat rims so that dry ingredient can be easily leveled. Spoons with deeper bowls are less likely to spill than those with narrow or wide and shallow bowls.

Mixing bowls: It's good to have both stainless steel and glass options to mix and hold prepped ingredients. Look for sets of nesting bowls ranging in capacity from 1¼ ounces to 4 quarts in glass and 2 cups to 8 quarts in stainless steel.

Parchment paper and baking mats: Non-stick surfaces are useful for baking crispy cookies without sticking to your trays. Parchment paper is oven-safe to 400°F (200°C) and keeps the bottom of the cookies from over-browning and sticking to the sheet. After baking, you can slide the parchment sheet with the baked cookies directly onto the cooling rack. Parchment paper can be reused several times and is easy to clean. You can even use parchment paper to improvise a pastry bag!

Pastry bags and piping tubes: Useful for piping cookie dough or adding icing to cookies. They come in many shapes and sizes, but a simple star-shaped tube and a plain tube are all you need to get great results.

Pastry wheel: Used to cut dough, these come with straight or fluted edges.

Pizzelle maker: A modern pizzelle maker is an electric appliance, much like a waffle maker. The batter is poured onto a nonstick finish, the lid is closed, and a snowflake-patterned flat waffle is the result. Some waffle makers include a pizzelle griddle.

Rolling pin: There are many choices, from nonstick to marble to those with ergonomic handles—the traditional American pin rolls on bearings. But many bakers prefer the French, stick-style tapered wood without handles. It easily turns and pivots, allowing you to feel the dough's thickness and apply pressure as needed. A pin 19-20 inches long is ideal for any rolling task.

Sieve or fine-mesh strainer: Use a strainer at least 6 inches in diameter for sifting flour and a small, fine-mesh sieve to sift powdered sugar over finished cookies as a decorative touch.

Spatula: Soft rubber or silicone spatulas are invaluable for scraping bowls, stirring batters, and folding egg whites. Large-bladed spatulas with stiff, relatively long handles with round edges are the most comfortable and efficient to use. Metal spatulas are used to lift cookies off sheet pans.

Stand mixer: For serious bakers, a stand mixer is virtually essential. They can handle nearly any task, from lightly whipping egg whites or cream to mixing heavy doughs and batters. Your mixer should have a powerful motor, a bowl of at least 4½ quarts in size, and include a flat paddle and dough hook.

Whisks: Also referred to as whips, these hand-held tools come in many styles. The French whisk is an excellent all-purpose tool. Longer and narrower than the standard round balloon whisk, it allows you to get closer to the sides of your bowl. The wires of any whisk should be slightly flexible.

Wire racks: Baking sheets taken right out of the oven cool better when placed on a wire rack. The rack allows air to freely circulate underneath, letting baked goods dry correctly.

Nana's Baking Tips

Preparing the Dough

Using a mixer: Unless otherwise directed by the recipe, beat the butter and sugar at high speed to blend into a light-colored, creamy mixture. Beat in the eggs and other liquid ingredients until the mixture is smooth and well-blended. Lower the speed or stir by hand with a sturdy wooden spoon to incorporate the flour. Do not overmix the dough, as it can result in tough cookies.

Using a food processor: Handy for flourless recipes, especially useful to grind nuts into paste or meal, but it typically cannot be used to make the dough.

Butter temperature: For the right cookie texture, the right butter temperature is crucial. If a recipe calls for softened butter, remove the butter from the refrigerator half an hour before baking. Do not use melted butter, as your cookies will spread too thinly and turn out heavy and greasy.

Home-made almond paste: Almond paste can be hard to find and expensive. Make your own. In a food processor, add 2 cups almond flour, 1 cup Confectioners' sugar, ¼ teaspoon salt. Pulse until combined. Add 2 egg whites and ½ teaspoon almond extract. Makes about 1 ¼ cups. Can store in the refrigerator for up to 10 days.

Creaming butter and sugar together: Cream butter at refrigerator temperature using an electric mixer or slightly softened if mixing by hand. Cream while gradually adding the sugar until the mixture appears light and fluffy. Be careful not to over-cream, or your butter-sugar mix will be too large in volume or too soft. If using a solid shortening instead, make sure it is at room temperature.

Whisking egg whites: Use a bowl that is completely clean and dry. Carefully separate the whites from the yolk, removing any yolk that dropped in with the whites.   Use large fine balloon whisk, beat until stiff peaks form, 4 – 5 minutes.

Toasting almonds: If the recipe calls for toasted nuts, be sure to toast them before adding them to the batter for maximum flavor. Taste them before using them to make sure they are not rancid. Place whole or sliced almonds in a single layer on an ungreased baking sheet. Bake at 350°F (180°C) for 8-10 minutes for whole almonds or 5-8 minutes for sliced almonds. Toss at least twice during the baking process, remove to a clean tray, and let cool 30 minutes before grinding.

Blanching hazelnuts: Skins from raw hazelnuts should be removed before using them in recipes. You can do this easily by toasting the hazelnuts on a baking sheet at 300°F (150°C) until fragrant and lightly toasted, 10-12 minutes. Let cool briefly, put them on a clean, flat-weave dish towel, and rub together vigorously.

Dried Fruit: To make chopping easier, freeze the fruit first. Before adding dried fruit to your batter, toss it with some of the same flour called for in the recipe. This keeps the fruit from sticking together and sinking to the bottom of the batter.

Rolling dough: If you do not want to roll dough on a floured surface, place dough between two large pieces of parchment paper before rolling with a rolling pin. No more sticky mess!

Making dough for pastry bags or pressed cookies: Working with dough for pressed or squeezed cookies can be a little tricky. The dough needs to flow smoothly through a cookie press or pastry bag. When making the dough, do not add all the flour called for in the recipe until you first test the dough by putting a small amount in the press or bag. The dough should be soft and pliable, not crumbly. Do not chill the dough — use it at room temperature. If dough becomes too soft, you can add 1-2 tablespoons of flour. But be careful: too much flour results in the cookie not spreading well when baked or becoming tough or crumbly. If the dough is too stiff, add the yolk of one egg.

Pastry bags: To improvise a bag, fold a piece of parchment paper into a cone. Load the dough inside the bag and twist the top closed. Snip a small hole at the cone end and squeeze dough onto a cookie sheet.

How to keep cookies from spreading: To keep cookies from spreading, chill the dough before baking. The protein content of flour is a major cause of flat cookies. Flour with a higher protein percentage (close to 13%) will help keep them from spreading.

Spacing between raw cookies: When placing cookies on a baking sheet, leave enough space between them, as most cookies will expand while baking. Unless otherwise indicated, leave 1 inch of space between small cookies and 2 inches of space between medium-sized cookies. Large cookies and loaves may need more space in between.

Baking the Cookies

Baking sheet preparation: To bake perfect cookies, start with a quality cookie sheet. Always wash before and after each use in warm soapy water. Rinse and thoroughly dry with a soft towel. Follow each recipe for specific sheet preparations.

With most cookie recipes, parchment paper is used to line the baking sheet. Parchment paper is oven-safe to 400°F (200°C) and reusable. A silicone baking mat is another option that is reusable and does not need greasing. Mats are oven-safe to 500°F (260°C).

If the recipe calls for the baking sheet to be greased instead, use a pastry brush or paper towel and solid vegetable shortening. Do not grease too generously, or your cookies will spread and over-brown. For best results, do not use butter, margarine, or liquid vegetable oil. You can also use a non-stick spray or cake release.

Always allow cookie sheets to cool completely between batches to prevent the dough from melting and spreading before baking. Washing will cool them down quickly.

Ovens: When was the last time you checked the accuracy of your oven temperature? The wrong temperature can leave your cookies doughy on the inside or over-browned and tough. To make sure your oven is at the proper temperature, purchase an inexpensive oven thermometer. One that mounts securely in the oven and has clearly marked numbers that make it easy to read quickly is best.

Convection oven: If using a convection oven, reduce the temperature by 10-15 degrees and reduce baking time by 1-2 minutes.

Preheating: Always preheat the oven and position your oven racks 10-15 minutes before you need to bake to ensure the cookies do not spread and lose their shape. It's best to bake only one sheet of cookies at a time on the middle rack in the center of the oven unless otherwise directed. Placing more than one sheet in the oven will reduce the oven temperature and block heat circulation. If you do bake two or more sheets at a time, switch cookie sheets front-to-back and top-to-bottom halfway through baking.

Over-baking: Try not to over-bake your cookies. Two minutes can make the difference between cookies that come out tough and hard, and cookies that are just perfect! For best results, oversee timing and bake just until set or very slightly browned. Since the bottoms of most cookies brown first, test when they are almost done by gently lifting the cookie with a spatula to check the bottom color. After checking for doneness, if necessary, bake them for a minute or two more. Remove the cookies from the oven when they still look a little underdone in their centers. They will finish cooking as they cool

Cooling cookies: Remove baked cookies from the oven. Place the cookie sheet on top of a rack for a minute or so to firm up slightly. Then move individual cookies to a rack to finish cooling. If the cookies are very delicate, let cool completely on the pan before removing them for storage.

Storing Cookies

Many bakers (including myself) desire to shove fresh-baked cookies in family's or friends' mouths and stomachs! But if you must store cookies elsewhere, keep them in an airtight container after they have completely cooled. Storage times will vary. When known for specific cookies, it is included with the recipe.

Room temperature: Generally, unglazed cookies can be kept at room temperature for 5-6 days. If glazed, they should be stored in a single layer for 3-4 days. In either case, if your home is very warm, refrigerating is a better choice. Tender cookies require a little extra care when storing to keep from crumbling or breaking - layer in an airtight container in between pieces of aluminum foil, waxed paper, or paper towels. To help cookies stay soft, you can put a slice of bread in the container. The bread will release moisture to keep the cookies moist, soft, and crumbly.

Freezing cookies: Many cookies and some doughs can be frozen in either a freezer bag or an airtight container. Some can stay for up to 3 months, although they may start to lose some flavor.

Measuring Ingredients

Follow all directions carefully. Dry ingredients should be measured in designated dry measuring cups, liquid ingredients in a clear, glass measuring cup.

Dry Ingredients: Use metal or plastic measuring cups for dry ingredients. If a recipe calls for a scant cup, measure the ingredient level, then remove two tablespoons. To measure teaspoons or tablespoons of dry ingredients like dip the exact-size measuring spoons into the can, then sweep off any excess with the back of a knife. For ⅛ teaspoon, measure ¼ teaspoon then cut through the middle with the point of a knife and push off the unneeded ⅛ teaspoon.

Flour: Stir flour lightly. Scoop using a large spoon into measuring cup until the cup is overflowing, then draw the back of flat knife across the top of the overflowing cup, sweeping off the excess. It is best not to press the flour down into the cup, scoop the flour up with the cup, nor tap the counter's measuring cup.

Granulated white sugar, flaky, or granular ingredients (i.e. cornmeal or coconut): With measuring cup, scoop the ingredient from the container, filling it to overflowing. Use the back of a knife to sweep off the excess.

Brown sugar and almond paste: Pack firmly into the appropriate cup with the back of a spoon and level off with back of a knife across the top.

Liquid Ingredients: Use a glass measuring cup for liquid ingredients. These cups have a handle and with markings dividing the cup into quarters and thirds. Place the cup on the countertop and pour in the liquid. Check amount at eye level.

Semi-Solid Ingredients: To measure semi-solids like ricotta cheese, use any cup measure, and spoon in the desired amount. To measure teaspoons or tablespoons of butter, sour cream, molasses, or other sticky substances, do not dip the spoon in — some will inevitably cling to the underside of the scoop, leaving you with more than you need. With liquids like melted butter, cream, syrups, and molasses, measure by pouring into a cup or spoon. For softened butter and sour cream, fill by packing it level with a knife.

Conversions

One cup in the US is different than one cup in many other countries. Recipes are written in US Standard units of measurement but can be converted to Gram or Metric for best accuracy. Use the following charts as a guide. All conversions are approximate and have been rounded up or down to the nearest whole number.

Volume Conversions

US	Metric
1 teaspoon	5 milliliters
1 tablespoon	15 milliliters
2 tablespoons	30 milliliters
⅛ cup (1 liquid ounce)	30 milliliters
¼ cup (2 liquid ounces)	59 milliliters
⅓ cup	79 milliliters
½ cup (4 liquid ounces)	118 milliliters
¾ cup	177 milliliters
1 cup (8 liquid ounces)	237 milliliters
1¼ cups	296 milliliters
1½ cups	355 milliliters
2 cups (16 liquid ounces)	473 milliliters
2½ cups	591 milliliters
3 cups	710 milliliters
4 cups (1 liquid quart)	0.946 liter
1.06 quarts	1.0 liter
4 quarts (1 liquid gallon)	3.8 liters

Weight Conversions

Ounces	Grams
½	14
¾	21
1	28
1½	43
2	57
2½	71
3	85
4	113
4½	128
5	142
6	170
7	198
8	227
9	255
10	283
12	340
16 (1 pound)	454

Temperature Conversions

In degrees Fahrenheit, water freezes at 32 degrees and boils at 212 degrees. In egrees Celsius, water freezes at 0 degrees and boils at 100 degrees. Since this will hange at elevations above sea level, you will need to learn how to adjust your gredients for high-altitude baking.

Oven Temperatures

Fahrenheit	Celsius
225	105
250	120
275	135
300	150
325	165
350	180
375	190
400	200
425	220

All the Cookies in the Jar

Nothing says home like freshly baked cookies. From the clatter of baking pans to the taste of fresh batter licked off the spoon to the aroma of a batch just out of the oven, cookies are a real feast for the senses. But they are much, much more. Have you ever choked up at the sight of that one special holiday cookie cutter or felt your mouth water at the memory of after-school treats still warm from the baking pan? In that case, you know that the most common cookie flavoring isn't chocolate or vanilla — it's nostalgia!

Cookies remind us of our parents and grandparents, who tempted us with their treats and, if we were lucky, passed on their secret recipes. They remind us of weddings and holidays shared with dear friends — or just average days made better and brighter with a little something sweet. They remind us of our family and our home. No wonder realtors perfume their listings with fresh-baked-cookie smells — nothing turns a house into a home like a batch of cookies.

Cookies, like homes, come in all shapes and sizes. Technically, cookies are small, crisp cakes made from sweetened dough. But cookies, of course, are anything but technical. They can be sweet or savory, tart or rich, crispy or chewy, studded with nuts or simple as sugar, frosted or plain, big or small. So, I prefer a looser, more romantic definition. If it reminds you of home, if the smell alone transports you, if one bite makes you close your eyes with pleasure, then it's probably a cookie. Still, it's useful to know a few basic types. Here are some of the most common.

Bar Cookies: Bar Cookies are usually made from a soft dough in a rectangular or square pan. Chewy or crisp, filled or layered, they are cut into squares or bars after baking.

Drop Cookies: Drop cookies are the most popular type of cookie and the easiest to make. As their name suggests, they are formed from balls of dough dropped onto a baking sheet. These mounds of dough flatten and spread during baking.

Molded (Shaped Cookies): Molded or shaped cookies are made from a stiff dough shaped by hand or with a mold before baking. Common shapes are balls, crescents, canes, logs, and wreaths. Balls can be flattened slightly with the bottom of a glass, a fork, or a molded pan to give them a new shape.

Pressed Cookies: Pressed cookies are made from soft pliable dough squeezed from a cookie press or pastry bag into decorative shapes. A cookie press can be fitted with various shaping disks such as stars, flowers, wreaths, and Christmas trees. Similarly, a pastry bag can take various metal tips or tubes and be held at different angles to create a variety of shapes.

Sliced Cookies: Sliced cookies (also called refrigerator or icebox cookies) are made from a stiff dough that is usually shaped into a roll then refrigerated. When thoroughly cold, the dough becomes hard enough to be sliced into round cookies and baked. Layers of different doughs can also be rolled together, spread with fillings, rolled into a log, sliced, and baked. This is an excellent prepare-ahead-of-time dough because it can be frozen, then sliced and baked as needed.

Rolled Cookies: Rolled cookies or cut-out cookies are made from a stiff dough that is chilled, then rolled out into a thick or thin sheet with a rolling pin, and then cut into a shape with a cookie cutter, pastry wheel, or knife.

No-Bake Cookies: As their name suggests, no-bake cookies don't require baking. They sometimes taste more like candy than a cookie because they are exceptionally rich in flavor.

Fried Cookies: Fried cookies are cooked by frying dough in vegetable oil. Often dusted with confectioners' sugar, they are best when served immediately.

Ricette di Famiglia

Cookie Recipes

From Family and Friends

Amaretti all'Amarena

Almond Cherry Macaroons

Oven Temp 300°F (150°C)　　　Bake 23-25 Minutes　　　Yields about 60 - 70

Ingredients

- 2½ pounds almond paste
- 6 large egg whites (about 1 cup)
- 2 cups granulated sugar
- 1 cup confectioners' sugar
- 2 tablespoons cornstarch
- Candied cherries (at least 36)

Directions

1. Preheat oven to 300°F. Line baking sheets with parchment paper.
2. In a large bowl, cut almond paste into small pieces size of peas.
3. Add dry ingredients and mix well.
4. In a separate bowl, beat egg whites until stiff.
5. Gently fold whites into batter. Hand mix well until there are no lumps.
6. Pass through cookie press using large star tip onto prepared baking sheets.
7. Cut cherries in half. Place one half in the center of each cookie.
8. Bake 23 – 25 minutes until lightly golden brown.
9. Let cool completely on the pan on cooling rack.

Storage:
Store in airtight container for up to 1 week. Can be frozen for up to 2 months.

Amaretti con Cioccolato

Almond Chocolate Cookies

Oven Temp 350°F (180°C)   Bake 17-20 minutes   Yields about 24

Ingredients:

- 1 ¼ cups almond paste
- ¾ cup granulated sugar
- 2 large egg whites, room temperature
- ½ cup confectioner's sugar
- 3 tablespoons Dutch-process cocoa powder
- ½ teaspoon almond extract

Directions:

1. Preheat oven to 350°F. Line 2 cookie sheets with parchment paper.
2. Crumble almond paste into a food processor.
3. Add sugar and pulse until evenly combined.
4. In separate bowl, beat egg whites till stiff peaks form
5. Add egg whites and extract to mixture. Fold in gently until incorporated.
6. Sift together confectioner's sugar and cocoa. Gradually add to almond mixture and mix well.
7. Drop by tablespoonfuls 2 inches apart onto prepared baking sheets.
8. Bake until tops are cracked, about 17-20 minutes. Cool for 1 minute before removing from pans to wire racks. Do not overbake.

Storage:
Store in an airtight container for up to 1 week. Can be frozen up to 2 months.

Ricciarelli

Almond Cookies, chewy

Oven Temp 300°F (150°C)   Bake 20 minutes   Yields about 20

Ingredients:

- 2 large egg whites
- 1 dash lemon juice
- 2¼ cups almond flour
- 1¾ cups confectioners' sugar
- 1 pinch salt
- ¼ teaspoon baking powder
- 1 teaspoon orange zest
- ½ of a large orange
- 1 tablespoon almond extract
- 1 teaspoon vanilla extract
- ½ cup confectioners' sugar for coating cookies

Directions:

1. Line 2 cookie sheets with parchment paper.
2. In a large bowl, sift together almond flour, 1¾ cups confectioners' sugar, salt, and baking powder.
3. In a separate mixing bowl, whip egg whites and lemon juice together until stiff peaks form.
4. Add egg whites to the almond mixture, folding in gently.
5. Add orange zest, vanilla extract, and almond extract. Fold in until combined.
6. Use clean hands, roll dough into balls about 1-inch in diameter, and then roll in confectioners' sugar until well coated.
7. Flatten cookies slightly with the palm of your hand into an oval shape. Place on prepared baking sheets with some space between them for spreading.
8. Leave at room temperature for about 1 hour, or until the tops have dried out and formed almost a little shell.
9. Pre-crack the shell by squeezing the cookies slightly from opposite corners. Pre-cracking will result in a beautiful white-gold contrast!
10. While cookies are drying, preheat oven to 300°F. When the cookies are ready, bake for about 20 minutes. Cool completely on a cooling rack.

Storage:
Store in an airtight container for up to 1 week.

Biscotti di Pizzo Amarato

Amaretto Lace Cookies

Oven Temp 350°F (180°C)   Bake 8 – 9 minutes   Yields about 16

Ingredients

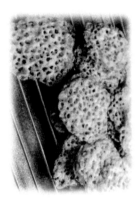

- 1/3 cup light brown sugar
- 2 tablespoons unsalted butter
- 1 tablespoon canola oil
- 1 tablespoon Amaretto (or orange juice)
- 1/4 cup almond meal
- 2 tablespoons cake or all-purpose flour
- 1/8 teaspoon salt

Directions

1. Preheat oven to 350°F. Prepare 2 baking sheets with parchment paper.
2. Combine brown sugar, butter, oil, and Amaretto in a bowl. Whisk together.
3. Microwave in 30-second increments for a total of one minute.
4. Add almond meal, flour, and salt. Stir to combine.
5. Scoop teaspoons of dough onto the prepared baking sheets; spaced 2-3 inches apart for spreading.
6. Bake 8-9 minutes, turning sheet halfway through. Allow to cool completely on the pan.

Storage:
Store up to 1 week in airtight container.

Biscotti all'Anice Glassati

Anise Cookies, glazed

Oven Temp 350°F (180°C)   Bake 10-12 minutes   Yields about 24 - 30

<u>Ingredients:</u>

Dough:
- 1½ cups plus 2 tablespoons all-purpose flour
- ½ teaspoon baking powder
- 1 teaspoon coarse salt
- 2 teaspoon ground anise
- 4 large eggs, room temperature
- 1 cup plus 2 tablespoons granulated sugar, plus more for sprinkling

Glaze:
- 1/4 cup milk
- 2 tablespoons butter, melted
- 1/2 teaspoon vanilla extract
- 2-1/2 cups confectioners'
- Optional - Food coloring

<u>Directions:</u>

Dough:
1. Preheat oven to 350°F. Line baking sheets with nonstick baking mats.
2. Sift flour, baking powder, salt, and anise together in a medium bowl.
3. Whisk eggs with a mixer on medium speed.
4. Slowly add sugar while increasing speed to high, and whisk until thick and glossy, about 10 minutes.
5. Reduce speed to low and add flour mixture, whisking until just combined.
6. Spoon batter into a pastry bag fitted with a ½-inch round tip.
7. Pipe 1-inch tapered mounds onto prepared baking sheets, spacing them 1 inch apart.
8. Bake until firm, 10 to 12 minutes. Let cool on sheets or wire racks.

Glaze:
1. In a small bowl, combine milk, butter, vanilla, and confectioners' sugar until smooth and relatively thick.
2. Tint with food coloring if desired.
3. When cookies are cool, spoon about ½ teaspoon glaze onto each cookie. Gently spread using the back of the spoon or a pastry brush. Let set at least 30 minutes.

Storage:
Already baked cookies can be frozen without the glaze. Freeze in an airtight plastic bag, squeezing out all the air. Defrost on the counter; glaze when at room temperature.

Store glazed cookies in airtight containers for up to a week. Layer with parchment paper, so glaze does not spread.

Pasta di Biscotto

Basic Cookie Dough
Nana's original recipe

Oven Temp 350°F (180°C)   Bake 10-15 minutes   Yields about 8 loaves

Ingredients:

Dough:
- 9½ cups flour
- 4 tablespoons baking powder
- 1 teaspoon salt
- 6 large eggs
- 1 cup granulated sugar
- ¾ cups whole milk
- 2 teaspoon vanilla extract
- 2 cups melted margarine

Filling suggestions:
- Any fruit preserve, spread in thin layer.
- Layer of brown sugar and walnuts, finely chopped.
- Thin layer of butter sprinkled with cinnamon.
- Combine 2 cups chopped apples with 1 cup strong coffee, 1 cup sugar, 1 cup raisins, 1 teaspoon cinnamon, ¾ teaspoon nutmeg, and ¾ teaspoon ground cloves. Let mixture cool completely and spread on dough.

Glaze:
- 1 cup confectioners' sugar
- 2-3 tablespoons fresh lemon juice

Directions:

Dough:
1. Preheat oven to 350°F. Line 2 baking sheets with parchment paper.
2. Sift together flour, baking powder, and salt in a large bowl.
3. In a separate bowl, beat together the eggs, sugar, milk, vanilla, and melted, cool margarine, till mixed.
4. Add egg mixture to the flour. Mix well and knead gently until all the flour is absorbed. Let stand 15 minutes or place in refrigerator for 30 – 60 minutes.
5. Divide dough into 8 equal sections.

6. Roll out dough one section at a time on a floured board to make rectangular shape 12 inch x 1/8 – 1/4 inch thick. Thinner is better. Chilled dough will be easier to handle.
7. Spread with nuts, fruit, or other fillings (see Filling Options).
8. From one end, fold over 2 or 3 times to form small loaves.
9. Place on prepared cookie sheet. Bake for 15 – 18 minutes or until lightly brown. Make sure inside layers are baked.
10. When cooled, frost with lemon frosting.

Lemon Glaze:
1. In medium bowl, whisk together confectioners' sugar, lemon flavoring or fresh lemon juice, and enough water to make a thin but runny glaze.
2. Spread or drizzle over completely cooled loaves.
3. Sprinkle with candy sprinkles or finely chopped nuts.

No Glaze Option:
Separate one large egg. Brush loaves with either egg white if you want shine or egg yolk.

Storage:
Store glazed loaves in airtight containers for up to four days. Layer with parchment paper, so glaze does not spread.

Already baked loaves can be frozen without the glaze. Freeze in an airtight plastic bag, squeezing out all the air. Defrost on the counter; glaze when at room temperature.

Biscotti di Mandorli

Biscotti - Almond

Oven Temp 375°F (190°C)   Baking Time 35-40 minutes   Yields about 36

Ingredients:

- ½ cup butter, softened
- 1 cup granulated sugar
- 3 large eggs, room temperature
- 1 teaspoon almond extract
- 2 cups all-purpose flour
- 2 teaspoons baking powder
- Pinch of salt
- ½ cup chopped almonds

Directions:

1. Preheat oven to 375°F. Line a baking sheet with parchment paper.
2. In a large bowl, cream butter and 1 cup sugar until light and fluffy, 5-7 minutes.
3. Add eggs, 1 at a time, beating well after each addition; add almond extract.
4. In a separate bowl, combine flour, baking powder, and salt. Gradually add to the creamed mixture until well mixed. Stir in almonds.
5. Divide dough in half, place on prepared baking sheet. Shape each in a 12-x-3-inch rectangle. Brush with milk and sprinkle with remaining sugar.
6. Bake until golden brown and firm to the touch, 15-20 minutes. Remove and allow to cool.

Second baking:
1. Reduce oven heat to 300 degrees.
2. Transfer loaves to a cutting board. Cut diagonally with a serrated knife into ½-inch slices. Place cut side down on ungreased baking sheets.
3. Bake for 10 minutes. Turn and bake until firm, 10 minutes longer. Remove to wire racks to cool.

Storage:
Store in an airtight container for up to 3 weeks.

Biscotti Doppio Cioccolato

Biscotti – Double Chocolate

Oven Temp 350°F (180°C)   Baking Time: 25-35 mins.   Yields 45 - 48

Ingredients:

- 4 ounces unsweetened bakers' chocolate
- 3 cups all-purpose flour
- 1 ½ teaspoons baking powder
- 1/8 teaspoon salt
- ½ cup butter, softened
- 1 cup granulated sugar
- 3 large eggs
- 1 teaspoon vanilla extract
- 2 teaspoons finely grated orange peel
- 1–1 ½ cups semisweet chocolate chips
- Optional: ½ cup semisweet chocolate chips for drizzling
- Vegetable oil for thinning

Directions:

1. Preheat oven to 350°F. Grease baking sheet or line with parchment paper.
2. Melt unsweetened chocolate in the top pan of a double boiler or the microwave. Set aside to cool.
3. In a medium bowl, whisk together the flour, baking powder, and salt. Set aside.
4. In a large bowl, with an electric mixer, cream together the butter and sugar.
5. Mix in the eggs one at a time. Add orange peel, vanilla, and melted chocolates. Stir/mix lightly.
6. Add dry ingredients and continue mixing until well blended.
7. Stir in chocolate chips till well combined.
8. On a lightly floured surface, divide the dough in half, and form two loaves about 11-inches x 2- inches. Place on prepared baking sheet.
9. Bake for about 20-25 minutes in a preheated oven or until they are firm to the touch. Allow to cool for 10 minutes.

Second baking:
1. With a serrated knife, cut diagonally into ½-inch slices.

2. Place slices cut side down back on the baking sheet. Bake an additional 5-10 minutes or until the cookies are golden in color and dry. Transfer to a cooling rack.
3. Melt semisweet chips in the top of a double boiler or the microwave; add a few drops of vegetable oil if needed to melt.
4. With biscotti on a parchment sheet or wax paper, drizzle or spread across one side. Allow to cool completely.

Storage:
Store in an airtight container for up to 1 week if drizzled with chocolate; up to 3 weeks plain.

Note: Butter makes it softer than traditional biscotti, so not suitable for dunking.

Biscotti Delle Festa

Biscotti – Holiday Cranberry Pistachio

Oven Temp 350°F (180°C)   Baking Time 49-55 minutes   Yields about 24

Ingredients:

- ½ cup butter
- 1 cup granulated sugar
- 3 large eggs
- 2 teaspoons vanilla extract
- 1 teaspoon orange extract
- 3 cups all-purpose flour
- ⅔ cup dried cranberries, coarsely chopped
- 2 teaspoons baking powder
- ½ teaspoon salt
- ⅔ cup pistachios, coarsely chopped
- 2 tablespoons grated orange zest

Directions:

1. Preheat oven to 350°F.
2. In a bowl, cream butter and sugar. Add eggs, one at a time, beating well after each addition. Stir in extracts.
3. Combine flour, baking powder, and salt. Gradually add to the creamed mixture and mix well (dough will be sticky).
4. Stir in cranberries, pistachios, and orange zest; cover the bowl with a cloth and chill for 30 minutes.
5. Divide dough in half. On a floured surface, shape each half into a loaf 1½ to 2 inches in diameter. Place on an ungreased baking sheet.
6. Bake for 30-35 minutes. Cool for 5 minutes.

Second baking:
1. Cut diagonally into ¾-inch-thick slices. Place slices cut side down on an ungreased baking sheet.
2. Bake for 9-10 minutes. Turn slices over. Bake for 10 additional minutes or until golden brown.
3. Cool on a wire rack.

Storage:
Store in an airtight container for up to 3 weeks.

Cantucci

Biscotti - Tuscan

Oven Temp 350°F (180°C)   Baking Time 30 minutes   Yields about 30

Ingredients:

- 3 cups all-purpose flour
- 1 teaspoon baking powder
- 7/8 cup granulated sugar
- 2 pinches of salt
- 3 large eggs + 2 egg yolks
- 1 tablespoon honey
- 1 teaspoon vanilla paste or extract
- 5 ounces whole almonds
- 2 tablespoons milk

Directions:

1. Preheat oven to 350°F.
2. In a large mixing bowl, add flour, baking powder, sugar, and salt. Whisk together by hand.
3. In a separate bowl, place 3 eggs and 1 egg yolk. Add honey. Whisk together by hand till blended
4. Add vanilla. Whisk again.
5. With a spoon, make a well in your flour mix. Pour egg mixture into the center of the well.
6. Stir with a spoon until the dough starts to come together. Finish mixing by hand till a dough is formed.
7. Add almonds. Knead until almonds are well combined into the dough.
8. Place dough on a floured surface. Form into a round shape. Cut dough into 2 equal halves.
9. Roll one section by hand until it forms a long roll about 11 inches long x 1 1/2 – 2 inches in diameter.
10. Place on the baking sheet. Repeat with other section.
11. In a small bowl, place yolk from the remaining egg.
12. Whisk till blended by hand. Apply to tops of both loaves with a pastry brush, coating generously.
13. Bake in preheated oven for 20 minutes. Let cool on pans for 10 minutes.

14. Cut diagonally into 1/2-inch slices. It may be a little crumbly as you slice through the loaf.
15. Place on baking sheets with sliced side up spaced 1/2 inch apart.

Second baking:
1. Reduce oven heat to 300 degrees.
2. Transfer loaves to a cutting board. Cut diagonally with a serrated knife into ½-inch slices. Place cut side up on ungreased baking sheets spaced 1/2 inch apart.
3. Bake for 10 minutes or until edges are browned, and tops are golden. Cool completely.

Traditionally dipped into Italian Vin Santo (Holy Wine), a sweet wine from Tuscany.

Storage

Store in airtight container for 3 – 4 weeks.

Ossi dei Morti

Bones of the Dead

Oven Temp 350°F (180°C)   Bake 20 minutes   Yields about 36

Ingredients:

- 2 cups all-purpose flour
- 2 cups granulated sugar
- 2 egg whites
- Juice of 1 lemon
- Pinch of cloves
- Pinch of cinnamon
- 4 ounces hazelnuts, lightly crushed
- 4 ounces almonds, lightly crushed

Directions:

1. Preheat the oven to 350°F. Line baking sheets with parchment paper.
2. In a large bowl, combine the flour, sugar, egg whites, and lemon juice.
3. Stir in the nuts. Knead dough until fairly firm.
4. Form dough into a ball. Cut into quarters.
5. Working with one section at a time, roll the dough out with your hands on a floured surface into a snake shape about ¼ - ½ inch wide.
6. Cut off 3-inch pieces and shape into "bones" with your hands. Should resemble a finger or leg bone.
7. Place on prepared baking sheets about 2 inches apart.
8. Bake about 20 minutes or until just starting to turn golden on the edges.
9. Cool completely before serving.

Storage
Store in airtight container for up to 1 week.

Occhi di Bue

Bull's Eye

Oven Temp 350°F (180°C)   Bake 11 – 12 minutes   Yields about 36

Ingredients:

- 1 cup granulated sugar
- 1 pound butter, unsalted
- 3 large egg yolks
- 3 cups all-purpose flour
- 1 tablespoon vanilla extract
- 1 pinch of salt
- 12 ounces apricot jam
- Confectioners' sugar for dusting

2 Cookie cutters: 1.5-inch Round & 3-inch Round

Directions:

1. In a large bowl, cream together butter and sugar with the tips of your fingers. Add egg yolks, flour, salt, and vanilla.
2. Knead together just until a smooth dough is formed. Shape into a ball.
3. Slightly flatten the dough, wrap in cling wrap. Refrigerate for at least 1 hour or overnight.

Assembly:
1. Knead the dough again until easy to handle. With a rolling pin, roll out on a floured surface until a thin 1/4-inch thick sheet.
2. Using a 3-inch cookie cutter, cut out round cookies. Place on prepared baking sheets. Knead again and roll out any leftover dough, and cut also.
3. In half the cookies, cut a round window with the smaller cookie cutter.
4. Bake in preheated oven for 11 – 12 minutes, until lightly golden.
5. Cool completed on wire cooling rack.
6. Place spoonful of jam on whole cookies. Cover with the window cookies.
7. Dust with confectioners' sugar.

Storage
Store in airtight container for 3-4 days, then refrigerate or freeze.

Biscotti al Burro

Butter Cookies

Oven Temp 350°F (180°C)   Bake 15 minutes   Yields about 40

Ingredients:

- 8 ounces butter, softened
- 1 cup confectioners' sugar or granulated sugar
- 2 large eggs
- 1 egg yolk, if needed
- 2 cups all-purpose flour, sifted
- 1 teaspoon baking powder
- 1 teaspoon vanilla extract
- Candied cherries
- Whole Almonds
- Chocolate kisses

Directions:

1. Preheat oven to 350°F. Line baking sheets with parchment paper.
2. In the electric mixer bowl, add butter and beat on medium speed until fluffy and light in color.
3. Add confectioners' sugar and beat until combined.
4. Add eggs and continue beating for 1-2 minutes until you get a fluffy, airy batter.
5. Using a kitchen spatula, fold in sifted flour, baking powder, and vanilla extract. Beat with mixer until batter is smooth, resulting in a fairly stiff dough.
6. Place dough in a cookie press or cloth pastry bag fitted with a large star tip.
7. Pipe onto prepared baking sheets about 1 inch apart. If the dough is too stiff to pipe, return to the bowl, add 1 egg yolk. Mix well and refill the press or pastry bag.
8. Place 1 candied cherry, whole almond, or chocolate kiss in the center of each cookie. Or melt chocolate and lightly drizzle over cookies.
9. Bake for about 15 minutes. Remove from oven. Let cool completely on the pan.

La Crema di Ricotta

Cannoli Ricotta Cream

Yields about 2 1/2 cups filling; enough for 20 small or 12 large shells.

Ingredients

- 1/2 cup whipping cream
- 15 ounces whole milk ricotta cheese, strained
- 1/2 cup confectioners' sugar
- 1/2 teaspoon vanilla extract
- 1/4 teaspoon ground cinnamon
- 1/3 cup mini dark chocolate chips
- Cannoli or Pizzelle shells 20 small or 12 large
- Optional: Pine nuts, chopped pistachios, chopped almonds

Directions

1. In bowl of stand or handheld mixer fitted with a whisk attachment, whip the cream until stiff peaks form. Place in a small bowl, set aside.
2. In the same mixing bowl, add the ricotta cheese, confectioners' sugar, vanilla, and cinnamon. Mix on medium speed until well combined, about 1 minute. Fold in the whipped cream and chocolate chips.
3. Chill the cream at least 2 hours before filling the cannoli shells.

Assembly:
1. Right before serving, fill a pastry bag with the cream filling. Or fill a medium-sized freezer bag with the filling; snip off the bottom corner to make a small hole for piping.
2. Pipe each shell from both ends until full.
3. Before serving, dust with confectioners' sugar. Serve immediately.

Optional: Instead of adding the chocolate chips to the cream, place chips or nuts on the cannoli' exposed ends after filling each shell.

Storage:
Plain pizzelles can be stored in an airtight container. Store empty cannoli shells in airtight container for up to 1 week. Store filling in the refrigerator in airtight container for up to 1 week. Assembled cannoli should be eaten immediately, as the filling will cause the shell to get soggy within 1 day.

Guanti, Wandi

Carnevale Fritters - Bow Ties

Electric Skillet - 375°F (190°C)   Fry till Golden Color   Yields about 48 - 60

Ingredients

- 6 large eggs
- ½ cup oil
- 1 cup granulated sugar
- 2 pounds all-purpose flour
- 3 teaspoons baking soda
- ½ teaspoon salt
- Zest of 1 lemon
- Oil for frying (vegetable or canola)
- Confectioners' sugar for dusting

Fluted pastry cutter

Directions

1. Whisk eggs and oil together in a medium bowl. Add sugar and mix with. Set aside.
2. In a large bowl, sift together flour, baking powder, and salt. Form a well in the center of the mix.
3. Pour egg mixture into center of well. Stir with a fork or by hand.
4. Knead until a soft, smooth dough forms. Let stand at least one-half hour.
5. Divide dough into baseball size balls. Roll each ball into a rectangular shape, very thin, about 1/8- inch thick.
6. Using a pastry cutting wheel, cut dough into 3-inch x 1 ½ inch strips.
7. In the center of each strip, make another cut lengthwise using the pastry cutter, stopping ¾ inch from each end. Take one end and fold under and bring the end up through the slit. Forms a "bow-tie."
8. Preheat oil in an electric skillet to 375°F.
9. Cookies will sink to the bottom at first. Once they float to the top, turn them over. Remove when a light golden butter color. Do not over-brown or will have a burnt flavor.
10. Drain on a paper towel. Dust with confectioners' sugar only before serving.

Storage:
Cookies are best served the same day. Store undusted in airtight container for up to 3-4 days. Can be frozen up to 2 months.

Cenci

Carnevale Fritters - Ribbons

Electric Skillet Temp 375°F (190°C)   Fry 1-2 minutes   Yields about 48

Ingredients:

- 3 large eggs
- 3 tablespoons granulated sugar
- ½ teaspoon salt
- ½ teaspoon vanilla extract
- 2 cups all-purpose flour
- 1½ teaspoon baking powder
- 1½ teaspoons butter, softened
- Oil for frying (vegetable or canola)
- Confectioners' sugar

Fluted pastry cutter

Directions:

1. In a bowl, beat eggs, sugar, and salt until frothy. Stir in vanilla.
2. Sift together flour and baking powder, and gradually add to the batter.
3. Add butter and mix well.
4. Turn out onto a floured surface and knead for 10 minutes.
5. Divide dough in half. Roll out each half as thin as possible (about ¼-inch thick).
6. Cut into 5-inch-x-1-inch strips with a knife or pastry wheel.
7. Preheat oil in an electric skillet to 375°F.
8. Fry cookies until golden brown, about 1 minute per side. Remove and drain on paper towels.
9. After cookies have cooled, sprinkle with confectioners' sugar.

Note:
Cookies are best served the same day. Store undusted in airtight container for up to 3-4 days. Can be frozen up to 2 months.

Lingua di Gato

Cat's Tongue

Oven Temp 375°F (190°C)   Bake 10-12 minutes   Yields about 25

Ingredients:

- 8 tablespoons butter, softened
- ¾ cup confectioners' sugar
- 3 large egg whites, room temperature
- 1 cup all-purpose flour
- 1 teaspoon vanilla

Directions:

1. Preheat oven to 375°F. Line 2-3 cookie sheets with parchment paper.
2. In a medium bowl, beat butter, confectioners' sugar, and vanilla until creamy.
3. Gradually add flour and continue beating.
4. Add egg whites one at a time. Beat until smooth and creamy. It should resemble cake frosting.
5. Fit a pastry bag with a ½-inch tip, fill with dough, and pipe out 3-inch-long strips, spaced about 1 inch apart.
6. Bake 10-12 minutes, or until lightly golden.
7. For the traditional flat shape, let cool completely on the pan. For a curved shape, wrap around a rolling pin while still hot. Cool completely.

Storage:
Can be stored for 2 weeks in an airtight container. Frozen for 1 month.

Biscotti Polenta all'Amarena

Cherry Cornmeal Spritz Cookies

Oven Temp 325°F (165°C)   Bake 10 minutes   Yields about 60 – 65

Ingredients:

- ½ cup granulated sugar
- 1/3 cup butter, softened
- 1/3 cup margarine *
- 2 large eggs
- 1 ½ teaspoon vanilla extract
- 1 teaspoon almond extract
- 1 cup all-purpose flour
- ⅔ cup yellow cornmeal
- Red candied cherries, halved

Cookie press with flower or star disk

Directions:

1. Preheat oven to 325°F. Prepare ungreased baking sheets or line with parchment paper.
2. In a bowl, cream butter and margarine and sugar until light and fluffy.
3. Beat in eggs and extracts.
4. In a separate bowl, whisk flour and cornmeal till combined.
5. Gradually beat flour mixture into the egg mixture.
6. Using a cookie press fitted with a flower or star disk, press dough 1 inch apart onto prepared baking sheets. Top with cherries.
7. Bake 9-11 minutes or until set. Remove from pans to wire racks to cool.

Storage:
Store in an airtight container for up to 1 week. Can be frozen for up to 2 months.

Note: Can use all butter if preferred.

Salame di Cioccolato

Chocolate Salami

No-Bake   Yields one log

Ingredients:
- 4½ ounces butter
- 2 eggs (or 50 mL milk)
- 1¾ ounces dark cocoa
- 5 ounces granulated sugar
- 1½ ounces rum, Amaretto, brandy, or orange juice
- 7 ounces tea biscuits, vanilla wafers, or another dry cookie
- Confectioners' sugar for dusting
- Optional: Crumbled almonds, hazelnuts, walnuts, and/or pistachios

Directions:
1. Melt butter over a very gentle heat. Remove from heat as soon as the butter has melted and let cool.
2. In a large mixing bowl, beat the eggs lightly.
3. Using an electric mixer, whisk together the cocoa, sugar, melted butter, and liquor. Add eggs (or milk). Continue whisking until you have a smooth and fluffy mixture that resembles a chocolate mousse.
4. Using a rolling pin, break up the biscuits into small pieces. Do not let them turn into powder.
5. Fold the biscuit pieces (and nuts, if using) into the chocolate mixture with a spatula until they are completely covered and well blended into the mix.
6. Pour out the chocolate mixture onto a large sheet of parchment or wax paper. Using two spatulas, form the mixture into a cylindrical shape resembling a salami log.
7. Roll up your Chocolate Salami in the paper, using your hands to smooth it out from end to end, then twist each end of the paper and tuck them under the salami. Chill in the refrigerator overnight to firm up.
8. Remove the salami from the fridge. Unwrap and dust it all over with confectioners' sugar.
9. Place Chocolate Salami on a cutting board, slice, and serve cold.

Storage:
Can be stored in an airtight container in the refrigerator for 3-4 days at most. Can be frozen, wrap in foil, for a maximum of 1 month.

Muzetta

Chocolate Spice Cookies

Oven Temp 375°F (190°C)   Bake 10 minutes   Yields about 24

Ingredients:

Dough:
- 4 cups all-purpose flour
- 1 cup granulated sugar
- 1 teaspoon baking soda
- ½ teaspoon baking powder
- ¼ teaspoon salt
- 4 heaping tablespoons cocoa
- ¼ teaspoon allspice
- ⅛ teaspoon cloves
- 1½ cups margarine, melted
- 1 cup milk
- 1 cup chopped walnuts

Chocolate Frosting:
- 1 cup confectioners' sugar
- 2 tablespoons cocoa
- 2 ounces margarine, softened
- Colored sprinkles

Directions:

1. Preheat oven to 375°F. Line cookie sheets with parchment paper.
2. Sift together flour, sugar, baking soda, baking, salt, cocoa, cinnamon, nutmeg, allspice, and cloves.
3. Stir in melted margarine and milk. Stir in walnuts. Let stand for 15 minutes.
4. Roll into 1-inch balls. Place on prepared cookie sheets. Bake 10 minutes.

Frosting:
1. In a medium bowl, mix together confectioners' sugar, cocoa, and softened margarine. Add a little water to thin if overly thick.
2. Drizzle chocolate in 2 different directions - OR - Dip cooled cookie upside-down into frosting bowl to cover top of cookie completely.

Storage:
Store in an airtight container for up to 4 days; freeze for a maximum of 1 month

Anginetti Natalizi

Christmas Lemon Ricotta Cookies

Oven Temp 375°F (190°C)   Bake 12-15 minutes   Yields about 24

Ingredients:

Dough:

- 2½ cups all-purpose flour
- 1 teaspoon baking powder
- 1 teaspoon salt
- 1 stick unsalted butter, softened
- 2 cups granulated sugar
- 2 large eggs
- 15 ounces whole-milk ricotta cheese
- 3 tablespoons lemon juice
- Zest of 1 lemon

Glaze:

- 2 teaspoons unsalted butter, melted
- 2 cups confectioners' sugar
- 1 tablespoon fresh lemon juice
- ½ teaspoon vanilla extract
- 2-3 tablespoons milk
- Optional: Red and green sprinkles

Directions:

Dough:

1. Preheat oven to 325°F. Line 2-3 cookie sheets with parchment paper.
2. In a medium bowl, combine the flour, baking powder, and salt. Set aside.
3. In the large bowl of an electric mixer, beat the butter and sugar until light and fluffy, about 3 minutes.
4. Add the eggs, 1 at a time, beating until incorporated.
5. Add the ricotta cheese, lemon juice, and lemon zest. Beat to combine.
6. Stir in the dry ingredients until well blended
7. Spoon the dough about 2 tablespoons at a time onto the prepared baking sheets, 2 inches apart.
8. Bake for 15 minutes, until slightly golden at the edges.
9. Remove from the oven and let the cookies rest on the baking sheet for 20 minutes.

Glaze:
1. In a mixing bowl, whisk together confectioners' sugar, melted butter, lemon juice, vanilla, and 2 tablespoons of milk until smooth. If too thick, can add in more milk, 1 teaspoon at a time. The glaze should be thick enough to coat the tops of cookies heavily.
2. When cookies are cool, spoon about ½ teaspoon glaze onto each cookie. Gently spread using the back of the spoon or a pastry brush. Immediately add sprinkles, if using.
3. Return cookies to wire rack.
4. Let the glaze harden for about 2 hours at room temperature.

Storage:
Can be stored for 1 week in an airtight container. Can be frozen for up to one month.

Mandorle di Citro

Citrus Almond Cookie

Oven Temp 325°F (165°C)   Bake 15 minutes   Yields about 72

Ingredients:

Dough:
- 4 cups unblanched almonds, toasted
- 1 cup granulated sugar
- 7-8 ounces milk chocolate bar
- 1 teaspoon ground cinnamon
- ½ teaspoon nutmeg
- 2 large eggs
- 4 tablespoons grated orange zest
- 3 teaspoons orange juice
- 2 teaspoon grated lemon zest
- 1 teaspoon lemon extract
- 2 teaspoons vanilla extract

Glaze:
- 1 cup confectioners' sugar
- ½ teaspoon lemon extract
- ½ teaspoon orange extract
- 1 teaspoon vanilla extract
- 2 - 3 teaspoons water

Directions:

Dough:
1. Place almonds in a food processor and process until chopped.
2. Finely dice the chocolate.
3. In large bowl, lightly mix the chopped almonds, sugar, chocolate, cinnamon and nutmeg until combined.
4. Using separate bowl, use mixer to gently beat the eggs, orange zest, orange juice, lemon zest, and extracts until mixed.
5. Gradually add egg mixture to almond mixture and mix well.
6. Cover and refrigerate for 2 hours or until easy to handle.
7. When the dough is chilled, preheat oven to 325°F. Line cookie sheets with parchment paper.

8. Roll dough into 1-inch balls. Place 2 inches apart on prepared baking sheets.
9. Bake for 12-15 minutes or until bottoms are lightly browned. Remove to a wire rack to cool.

Glaze:
1. In a small bowl, combine the confectioners' sugar, extracts, and enough water to achieve spreading consistency. Glaze should run off the spoon slowly, a little thicker than a glazed doughnut.
2. Spread or drizzle over completely cooled cookies

Storage:
Store in an airtight container for up to one week.

Mostaccioli

Citrus Spice Cookies

Oven Temp 350°F (180°C)   Bake 10 minutes   Yields about 72

Ingredients:

Dough:
- 3 cups all-purpose flour
- 2 cups almonds
- 1/3 cup baking cocoa powder
- 1/4 teaspoon ground cloves
- 1/2 teaspoon cinnamon
- 2 teaspoons baking powder
- pinch of salt
- 4 large eggs
- 1 1/2 cup granulated sugar
- 1 large orange, zested
- 1 medium lemon, zested
- 1/2 teaspoon pure vanilla extract
- Juice of 1 lemon
- 3 ounces coarsely grated semisweet or bittersweet chocolate

Chocolate Coating
- 12 ounces semisweet or bittersweet chocolate
- 12 ounces white chocolate
- vegetable oil for thinning the chocolate

Cookie-cutter: 2-inch Diamond shape

Directions:

1. Preheat the oven to 350°F. Line 4 cookie sheets with parchment paper and set aside.
2. In a large bowl, whisk together the flour, finely ground almonds, cocoa powder, cloves, cinnamon, baking powder, and salt. Set aside.
3. In a separate large bowl, using a stand mixer or handheld mixer, beat the eggs together.
4. Mix in the sugar and honey, beating until very well combined.
5. Stir in the orange and lemon zest, vanilla extract, and lemon juice.
6. Slowly mix in the flour mixture until combined.

7. Stir in the grated chocolate. The dough should be very soft and pliable.
8. Working with small portions of the dough (about 1 heaping cupful), transfer to a well-floured surface.
9. With a floured rolling pin, roll out the dough to about 1/3 inch thick.
10. Dip a 2-inch diamond cookie cutter into some extra flour on your work surface and use it to cut out the diamond-shaped cookies. Gently lift with metal spatula and place on prepared baking sheet spaced about 1 inch apart.
11. Bake in the preheated oven for about 10 minutes; it should still be slightly soft to the touch when ready. Remove and set on a cooling rack for a few minutes, then transfer each cookie to a cooling rack to complete cooling.
12. Repeat with the remaining dough.

Chocolate Coating
1. When cookies are completely cool, melt the semisweet chocolate using a double boiler or in the microwave, using a microwave-safe bowl on high for about 90 seconds, stirring at 30-second intervals.
2. Thin the chocolate with a small amount of vegetable oil will make for easy dipping.
3. Dip half a batch of the cookies into the melted semisweet chocolate. Place on a cooling rack till the chocolate sets.
4. Repeat by melting the white chocolate and coating the remaining cookies.
5. Before the white chocolate sets, use a piping bag filled with dark melted chocolate to dot the tops, then simply run a toothpick through the dots to create a pretty pattern.
6. Allow for the chocolate to set completely before storing.

Storage:
Store in an airtight container for up to 1 week. Can be frozen for up to 2 months.

Krumiri

Crooked Moustache

Oven Temp 325°F (165°C)   Bake 15 minutes   Yields about 48 - 60

Ingredients:

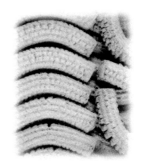

- 1 1/2 cups all-purpose flour
- 1 cup very fine yellow cornmeal
- 1 cup unsalted butter, cold
- 2/3 cup granulated sugar
- 1 teaspoon vanilla extract
- 3 large egg yolks

Directions:

1. Preheat oven to 325°F. Prepare 2–3 baking sheets lined with parchment
2. In a medium bowl, stir the flour and cornmeal together till well mixed. Set aside.
3. In a large bowl, cut butter into pieces. Add sugar and cream together with mixer set at medium speed. Continue beating until the mixture lightens in both texture and color, 4 to 5 minutes.
4. Beat in the vanilla, then the egg yolks one at a time, beating smooth after each addition.
5. Add the flour mixture, stir with a large spatula, and then finish mixing by hand till well blended.
6. Using a pastry bag fitted with a 1/2-inch star tip, pipe the dough onto prepared baking sheets in slightly curved shapes about 4 inches long. Or straight but slightly crooked like a mustache.
7. Bake the about 15 minutes till golden. Remove from pans and cool on a rack.

Storage:
Store in an airtight container for up to 1 week. Can be frozen for up to 1 month.

Taralli Dolci di Pasque

Easter Cookies

Oven Temp 350°F (180°C)   Bake 10-15 minutes   Yields about 32

<u>Ingredients:</u>

Dough:
- 5½ cups all-purpose flour
- 1½ tablespoons baking powder
- 6 large eggs
- 1¼ cups granulated sugar
- 3/4 cup unsalted butter
- 2 tablespoons vanilla

Icing:
- 3 cups confectioners' sugar
- 4 tablespoons water
- ½ teaspoon lemon extract or ⅛ teaspoon Fiori di Sicilia
- Nonpareil sprinkles

<u>Directions:</u>

Dough:
1. Melt the butter over very gentle heat. Do not burn the butter. Remove from heat and let cool.
2. In a large bowl, whisk together flour and baking powder.
3. In the bowl of an electric mixer, whisk the eggs, then beat in the sugar.
4. Mix in the melted butter and vanilla.
5. Gradually add in the flour mixture to form a soft dough.
6. Refrigerate the dough for at least 1 hour or overnight, until firm enough to handle.

Assembly:
1. When ready to bake, preheat oven to 350°F. Line a baking sheet with parchment paper.
2. Divide dough into 32 even pieces.
3. Roll each dough piece into a ball, then into a 7-inch rope. Press the ends of the rope together to form a circle.
4. Place dough rings on baking sheet 2-3 inches apart.
5. Bake for 10-14 minutes, until puffed and just turning golden.

6. Cool completely on wire racks before icing.

Icing:
1. Have cookies and nonpareil sprinkles ready.
2. In a small saucepan over low heat, stir confectioners' sugar, water, and extract just until combined and barely warm.
3. Dip the cookie tops into the icing or use a pastry brush to coat the cookies with icing, and immediately add the sprinkles.

Note:
This icing hardens very quickly and must be used immediately. It's helpful if one person ices while a second person adds the sprinkles before the icing hardens. Once the icing in the saucepan hardens, do not try to reheat it. The sugar will crystallize and turn sandy.

Storage:
Store cookies in an airtight container at room temperature for up to 7 days.

Florentino

Florentines

Oven Temp 350°F (180°C)   Bake 10 - 11 minutes
Yields about 60 (3-inch) or 30 (6-inch)

Ingredients:

Dough:
- 1 ¾ cups blanched almonds
- 3 tablespoons all-purpose flour
- 1 orange zest, finely grated
- ¼ teaspoon fine salt
- ¾ cup granulated sugar
- 2 tablespoons heavy cream
- 2 tablespoons light corn syrup
- 5 tablespoons unsalted butter
- ½ teaspoon vanilla extract

Optional - Chocolate topping:
- 2 – 4 ounces semisweet chocolate

Directions:

Dough:
1. Preheat oven to 350°F. Line baking sheets with parchment paper.
2. In a food processor, pulse the almonds until finely chopped but not pasty.
3. In a large bowl, stir together the almonds, flour, zest, and salt.
4. In a small saucepan, add the sugar, cream, corn syrup, and butter. Cook over medium heat, stirring often until the mixture comes to a rolling boil and sugar is completely dissolved. Continue to boil for 1 minute. Remove from heat and stir in vanilla. Pour mixture into almond mixture; stir just to combine. Set aside until cool enough to handle, about 30 minutes
5. For 3-inch cookies, scoop rounded **teaspoons** of batter. To make 6-inch cookies, scoop rounded **tablespoons** of batter. Roll into balls and place on prepared baking sheets, leaving 3 - 4 inches between each cookie.
6. Bake one sheet at a time in the center rack of oven for about 10 – 11 minutes. Rotate the baking sheet halfway through baking time.
7. Cool on baking sheet for 5 minutes, then transfer to racks to cool. Serve.

Optional Chocolate topping:
1. Place chocolate in a medium heat-proof bowl. In a saucepan filled with 1-inch or more of water to a very low simmer. Set the bowl of chocolate over but not touching the water. Stir often until melted and smooth. Or can melt chocolate in a medium microwave-safe bowl. Microwave at 50 percent power until soft, about 2-3 minutes, stirring once halfway through.
2. Spread melted chocolate over Florentines, covering one side completely. Cool at room temperature until chocolate is set.
3. Serve upside down.

Storage:
Store carefully in an airtight container, separated by parchment or waxed paper, for up to 3 days. Keep separated from moist cookies or baked goods. Can be frozen in layers between wax paper up to 2 months.

Biscotti Ripieni di Frutta

Fruit Filled Spritz Cookies

Oven Temp 375°F (190°C)   Bake 12-15 minutes   Yields about 84 – 90

Ingredients:

Filling:
- 1-1/2 cups chopped dates
- 1 cup water
- 1/2 cup granulated sugar
- 2 teaspoons orange juice
- 2 teaspoons grated orange zest
- 1 cup maraschino cherries, chopped
- 1/2 cup sweetened shredded coconut
- 1/2 cup ground nuts (hazelnuts and/or walnuts)

Dough:
- 1 cup butter, softened
- 1 cup granulated sugar
- 1/2 cup packed brown sugar
- 3 large eggs, room temperature
- 1/2 teaspoon almond extract
- 1/2 teaspoon vanilla extract
- 4 cups all-purpose flour
- 1/2 teaspoon baking soda
- 1/2 teaspoon salt
- Optional: Confectioners' sugar

Directions

Filling:
1. In a small saucepan, combine the dates, water, sugar, orange juice, and orange zest. Bring to a boil, stirring constantly. Reduce heat; cook and stir for 8 minutes or until thickened.
2. Cool completely. Stir in the cherries, coconut, and nuts; set aside.

Dough:
1. In a large bowl, cream butter, granulated and brown sugars until light and fluffy, 5-7 minutes.
2. Beat in eggs and extracts.

3. In a separate bowl, combine the flour, baking soda, and salt. Gradually add to the creamed mixture and mix well.
4. Using a cookie press fitted with a bar disk, press a 12-in.-long strip of dough onto an ungreased baking sheet.
5. Spread fruit filling over dough. Press another strip over the filling.
6. Cut into 1-in. pieces, can remain unseparated. Repeat with remaining dough and filling.
7. Bake for 12-15 minutes or until edges are golden. Recut into pieces if necessary.
8. Remove to wire racks to cool. Dust with confectioners' sugar if desired.

Storage:
Can store at room temperature in an airtight container for up to 1 week. Can be frozen in layers between wax paper up to 2 months.

Noci Di Burro

Hazelnut Butter Cookies

Oven Temp 350°F (180°C)   Bake 15-20 minutes   Yields about 40

Ingredients:

- 1 cup plus 1 tablespoon **salted** butter, softened
- 1/2 cup granulated sugar
- 2 cup all-purpose flour
- 4.25 ounces whole hazelnuts
- 40 whole hazelnuts
- 3 ounces whole milk
- 2 large egg yolks
- 2 teaspoons vanilla

Directions:

1. Preheat oven to 350°F. Line cookie sheets with parchment paper.
2. Roast all hazelnuts for 5-6 minutes. Remove skins by rubbing with a tight weave towel.   Move to a clean bowl. Remove 40 hazelnuts and set aside.
3. Place the remaining hazelnuts in a food processor and pulse until finely chopped. Set aside.
4. In a separate bowl, using a mixer, cream the butter and sugar together until fluffy, 2-3 minutes.
5. Add the flour, chopped nuts, egg yolk, milk, and vanilla. Mix until just combined into a dough.
6. Drop by teaspoonfuls onto the prepared cookie sheets.
7. Place a whole roasted hazelnut on each cookie round.
8. Bake for 15-20 minutes, or until golden.
9. Let cool 10-15 minutes on the cookie sheet, then move to a wire rack to cool completely.

Storage:
Store cookies in an airtight container at room temperature for up to 7 days.

Tricolore

Italian Flag - Venetian Torts

Oven Temp 350°F (180°C)   Bake 8-10 minutes
Yields about 8 bars (80 slices)

Ingredients:

- 1 pound almond paste (1½ cups)
- 3 cups margarine, softened
- 8 large eggs, separated
- 2 cups granulated sugar
- 2 teaspoons almond extract
- 4 cups flour
- ½ teaspoon salt
- 30 drops each red and green food coloring

Filling and Chocolate coating:
- 22 ounces apricot or raspberry preserves
- 24 ounces of chocolate chips

Directions:

1. Preheat oven to 350°F. Grease two 13-x-9-x-2-inch pans. Line with waxed paper, leaving a 2-inch overhang on both ends. Grease the waxed paper.
2. In a large bowl, break up almond paste into small bits.
3. Add egg yolks, margarine, sugar, and extract. Beat mixture with an electric mixer until smooth, 3-5 minutes.
4. Add flour and salt, mixing well.
5. Beat egg whites in a separate bowl until stiff. Fold half into the batter, stirring gently to lighten. Fold in remaining whites and blend well.
6. Divide batter evenly into three bowls. Stir green food coloring into one bowl, red food coloring into the second bowl, and leave the third bowl plain.
7. Pour green batter into prepared pan, spreading evenly, about ¼ inches thick.
8. Bake 8-10 minutes, until just set and slightly golden. It may appear under-baked — use a toothpick to test. Nana says, "If it comes out clean, it's ready."

9. Using the paper overhangs, transfer the layer to a wire rack to cool for 15 minutes. Repeat the process with the plain layer and the red layer.

Assembly:
1. When all layers are cool, invert the green layer onto a large baking sheet lined with parchment or wax paper. Spread layer with half of the preserves.
2. Invert the white layer on top of the green layer and spread with remaining preserves.
3. Invert the red layer on top of the white layer.
4. Wrap all three layers together on the tray with plastic wrap. Place a heavily weighted baking pan on top to compress and compact layers. To weight pan: place sack of flour, beans in bags, rice in bags, or other items to add weight to the pan. I've known some Italians to use bricks. Chill at least 8 hours or overnight.
5. Remove weight and plastic wrap. Trim edges of assembled layers with a long, serrated knife. Carefully cut crosswise into 8 even bars, with each bar approximately 1½-x-9 inches.

Chocolate Coating:
1. Melt chocolate in a double boiler or microwave. Frost each bar on all surfaces except the bottom.
2. Place in the refrigerator to set.
3. Once the chocolate has cooled and set, score the top into ¾-inch slices and wrap in freezer paper.
4. Freeze. This makes it easier to slice when ready to serve without crumbling the chocolate.

Storage:
Store in freezer for up to 2 months. Remove and let come to almost room temperature before serving.
Store bars in the refrigerator for up to 1 week.

Savoiardi

Lady Fingers

Oven Temp 390°F (200°C)   Bake 8 - 12 minutes   Yields about 36

Ingredients:

- 4 large eggs, separated
- ½ cup + 1 tablespoon granulated sugar
- 5 1/3 tablespoon cornstarch
- ¾ cup + ½ tablespoon all-purpose flour
- 1 teaspoon vanilla extract
- 4 tablespoons confectioners' sugar

Directions:

1. Preheat oven to 390°F. Line baking sheets with parchment paper.
2. Beat the egg whites, then beat in cornstarch and half the granulated sugar until the mixture forms a stiff meringue.
3. In a separate bowl, beat the egg yolks with remaining sugar and vanilla extract.
4. Fold in flour and beaten egg whites mix.
5. Using a pastry bag with a plain 1/2-inch tip, pipe the batter onto the prepared baking sheets spacing 1 inch apart.
6. Sprinkle ladyfingers with confectioners' sugar.
7. Bake 8-12 minutes until the cookies are lightly colored. Do not over-brown.
8. Place baking sheet on a cooling rack. Let cookies cool completely before removing them.

Storage:
Store cookies in an airtight container at room temperature for up to 7 days.

Baci di Dama

Lady Kisses

Oven Temp 350°F (180°C)   Bake 16-18 minutes   Yields about 40

Ingredients:

- 1 cup hazelnuts, toasted and skinned
- ¼ cup granulated sugar
- ½ cup all-purpose flour
- 2 tablespoons cornstarch
- ¼ teaspoon salt
- 5 tablespoons unsalted butter, cold
- ½ teaspoon vanilla extract

Filling:
- ½ cup bittersweet chocolate chips (about 3 ounces) or substitute Nutella

Directions:

1. Place the hazelnuts, flour, sugar, cornstarch, and salt in a food processor and process until finely ground, about 30 seconds.
2. Cut cold butter into small pieces. Add with vanilla to mix. Pulse until dough comes together.
3. Divide the dough into 4 equal parts. Wrap each piece in cling wrap. Refrigerate for 2 hours or more, until very cold and firm.
4. Line 2 cookie sheets with parchment paper. Remove 1 disk of dough, keeping others refrigerated.
5. Press and roll dough into a 10-by-1-inch rope. Cut into 20 pieces, ½-inch each.
6. Roll each piece into a small ball and place on prepared sheets. Space about 1 ½ inch apart.
7. After filling the first sheet, place it in the refrigerator. Repeat the process until all dough is used.
8. Chill rolled cookies for about 1 hour, or, if in a hurry, freeze for ½ hour.
9. When ready to bake, preheat the oven to 350°F.
10. Bake one sheet at a time for 13-15 minutes, or until light golden brown.
11. Set cookie sheet onto a cooling rack.
12. Repeat with the second cookie sheet.

13. Let the cookies cool completely on sheets before filling with the melted chocolate.

Assembly:
1. Melt chocolate chips in a microwave-safe bowl at 50% power, occasionally stirring, until melted, 1-2 minutes.
2. With a spoon, put a dollop of chocolate (about ¼ teaspoon) on the flat side of each cookie.
3. Top with a second cookie and press down slightly to form a sandwich.
4. Let chocolate set before serving, about 15 minutes.

Storage:
Store in airtight container 3 – 5 days.

Anginetti

Lemon Cookies

Oven Temp 320°F (160°C)　　　Bake 15 minutes　　　Yields about 24

Ingredients:

Dough:

- 1¼ cups all-purpose flour
- ¼ cup plus 2 tablespoons cornstarch
- ¼ teaspoon salt
- Zest and juice of one lemon (about 2 tablespoons)
- ¾ cup plus 2 tablespoons unsalted butter, softened
- ½ cup confectioners' sugar

Lemon Glaze:
- 3 tablespoons fresh lemon juice, strained
- 1½ cups confectioners' sugar
- Zest of 1 lemon

Directions:

Dough:
1. In a medium bowl, whisk together flour, cornstarch, zest, and salt.
2. In the bowl of an electric mixer, beat butter and confectioners' sugar on medium speed until fluffy, 3-5 minutes.
3. Add half the flour and the lemon juice and beat to combine. Add the remaining flour and, using a wooden spoon or spatula, combine to form a dough. The dough should be a little sticky. Add a tablespoon or two of flour if it is too sticky to handle.
4. Transfer dough to a large piece of parchment paper and roll into a log approximately 1½ inches wide. Wrap in parchment paper and refrigerate for 1 hour.
5. Line baking sheets with parchment paper.
6. Remove the dough from the refrigerator and cut into ½-inch slices. Place slices on prepared baking sheets; refrigerate for another 20 minutes.
7. Preheat oven to 320°F. Bake for 5 minutes

8. Raise oven temperature to 350°F (180°C) and continue to bake for 9-10 minutes, or until light gold in color.
9. Remove from the oven and let sit for five minutes. Transfer cookies to a wire rack to cool completely.
10. Cookies can either be dusted with confectioners' sugar or spread with a lemon glaze.

Lemon Glaze:
1. In a small bowl, whisk together lemon juice, confectioners' sugar, and zest until smooth.
2. Spread or drizzle on cooled cookies.

Storage:
Store in airtight container 3 – 5 days. Can be frozen for up to 1 month.

Anginetti

Lemon Crinkle Cookies

Oven Temp 375°F (190°C)   Bake for 10-12 minutes   Yields about 50

Ingredients:

- ⅔ cup almond flour
- 1¼ cups all-purpose flour
- ½ cup granulated sugar
- 1 tablespoon baking powder
- Zest and juice of 1 lemon (about 4 ounces)
- 4 ounces butter, cold, cut into cubes
- 1 large egg
- ½ cup confectioners' sugar

Directions:

1. In a food processor, add almond flour, all-purpose flour, baking powder, sugar, and lemon zest. Pulse a few times.
2. Add butter and pulse until you get a crumbly dough.
3. Mix in egg and lemon juice.
4. Knead briefly until all ingredients are well combined.
5. Wrap the dough with plastic wrap and let rest in the refrigerator for 20-30 minutes.
6. Preheat oven to 375F. Line 2-3 baking sheets with parchment paper.
7. Cut off a small piece from the dough ball and roll it into a rope approximately ½-inch thick. Cut the rope into ½-inch pieces.
8. Quickly roll each piece between your palms, forming a ball shape.
9. Roll balls in confectioners' sugar and place on baking sheets, about 1½ inch apart. Leave round or flatten tops slightly to crack cookie tops.
10. Bake for 10-12 minutes. Remove when still pale and only lightly brown on the edges.

Storage:
Store in airtight container for up to 1 week. Can be frozen for 1 to 2 months.

Canestrelli

Little Baskets - Egg Yolk Cookies

Oven Temp 335°F (170°C)   Bake 15 minutes   Yields about 36

Ingredients

- 4 large egg yolks, hard-boiled
- 1 1/4 cup all-purpose flour
- 1 cup + 1 teaspoon cornstarch
- 1 cup cold butter
- 2/3 cup confectioners' sugar
- Zest of 1 lemon
- 1 teaspoon vanilla extract

Cookie-cutter: 2-inch Flower shape

Directions

PREP: Place eggs in a pot of cold water and bring it to boil. Reduce heat to medium; cook 8-10 minutes, depending on altitude. Place in cold water to cool.   Peel, remove egg yolk, set egg yolks in the refrigerator to cool.

1. In a large bowl, sift together flour, cornstarch, and confectioners' sugar.
2. Add lemon zest, vanilla, and cold butter cut in cubes.
3. Mix all with a dough blender or in a food processor.
4. Grate cold egg yolks; add to mix.
5. Knead the dough by hand until it comes together in a smooth ball.
6. Cover with a plastic wrap and set aside to rest for about 30-60 minutes or refrigerate overnight. Take the dough out at least 1 hours before assembly.

Assembly:
1. Preheat oven to 335F. Line 2-3 baking sheets with parchment paper.
2. Cut off a large piece of the dough. On a lightly floured work surface, roll it out 1/3-inch thick.
3. Using a flower-shaped cookie cutter, cut out the cookies. Press out the center of the cookie with a straw or other small round hollow tool.
4. Transfer cookies onto prepared baking sheets.
5. Bake for 10-15 minutes. Cookies should remain pale, not brown.
6. Let cookies cool completely on a wire rack.
7. Dust generously with confectioners' sugar.

Storage:
Store up to 1 week in airtight container. Can freeze up to 2 months.

Pizzicati

Pinched Cookies - Italian Horns

Oven Temp 350°F (180°C)   Bake 10-12 minutes   Yields about 60

Ingredients:

- 1 cup cold butter, cubed
- 4 cups all-purpose flour
- 2 cups vanilla ice cream, softened
- 12 ounces cherry filling
- Granulated sugar, for sprinkling
- Optional: Confectioners' sugar

Fluted pastry cutter

Directions:

1. In a large bowl, cut butter into the flour until mixture resembles coarse crumbles.
2. Stir in ice cream.
3. Divide into 4 portions. Cover and refrigerate for at least 2 hours or overnight.

Assembly:
1. Preheat oven to 350°F. Prepare 2 ungreased baking sheets or line with parchment paper.
2. On a lightly floured surface, roll each portion ⅛ inch thick. With a fluted pastry cutter, cut into 2-inch squares.
3. Place about ½ teaspoon of filling into the center of each square. Fold corners of dough over the filling and seal. Sprinkle lightly with sugar.
4. Place on prepared baking sheets.
5. Bake for 10-12 minutes, or until bottoms are light brown.
6. Cool on wire racks. Dust with confectioners' sugar if desired.

Storage:
Store in airtight container for up to 3 days. Refrigerate up to 1 week.

Pignoli

Pine Nut Cookies

Oven Temp 325°F (165°C)   Bake 15-18 minutes   Yields about 30

Ingredients:

- 1¼ cups almond paste (12 ounces)
- ½ cup granulated sugar
- 4 large egg whites, room temperature (separated by 2s)
- 1 cup confectioners' sugar
- 1½ cup pine nuts

Directions:

1. Preheat oven to 325°F. Line 2 or 3 cookie sheets with parchment paper.
2. In a medium mixing bowl, beat almond paste and sugar until crumbly.
3. Gradually beat in 2 of the 4 egg whites.
4. Add confectioners' sugar gradually. Mix well.
5. Whisk the remaining 2 egg whites in a shallow bowl. Place pine nuts in another shallow bowl.
6. Shape dough into 1-inch balls. Roll in egg whites and coat with pine nuts.
7. Place 2 inches apart on prepared baking sheets. Flatten slightly
8. Bake until lightly browned, 15-18 minutes.
9. Cool for 1 minute before removing from pans to wire racks.

Storage:
Can be stored for 1 week in an airtight container.

Amaretti Stelle di Ananas

Pineapple Stars

Oven Temp 425°F (220°C)   Bake 10 minutes   Yields about 140

Ingredients:

Dough:

- 6 large eggs
- 2 cups granulated sugar
- 1½ cups margarine
- 4 tablespoons baking powder
- 1 teaspoon vanilla extract
- 9 cups flour
- 1 teaspoon salt
- Pineapple preserves

Lemon Icing:
- 3 cups confectioners' sugar
- 3 - 4 tablespoons water
- ½ teaspoon lemon extract or ⅛ teaspoon Fiori di Sicilia
- Small colored sprinkles or decorating sugars

Directions:

Dough:
1. Preheat oven to 425°F.
2. In a large bowl, sift together flour, baking powder, and salt. Set aside.
3. In a separate bowl, beat eggs. Add sugar and beat until fluffy.
4. Add melted margarine and continue beating. Add vanilla extract.
5. Add this mixture to the dry ingredients and mix slowly for about 1 minute or until thoroughly blended.
6. Place dough in a cookie press using the star shape and onto an ungreased cookie tray. Do not crowd cookies. (See **Nana's Baking Tips** on Making Dough for…. Pressed Cookies)
7. Use your thumb to press down the middle of each cookie, making a small circular indent.
8. Place ½ teaspoon pineapple preserves in each.

9. Bake for 10 minutes or until golden, very lightly browned. Do not over bake.
10. Frost while still warm. Shake colored sprinkles on top.

Lemon Icing:
1. Mix confectioners' sugar, lemon flavoring, and enough water to make a thin but not runny icing.
2. Use a pastry brush to coat the cookies with icing.
3. Immediately sprinkle tops of cookies with colored sprinkles or sugars.

Storage:
Store for 1 week in an airtight container. Can be frozen for up to 2 months.

Pizzelles - Cannoli Pizzelles

Pizzelles & Cannoli Pizzelles

Electric Pizzelle Maker   Yields about 60

Ingredients

- 6 large eggs
- 3 ½ cups flour
- 1 ½ cups granulated sugar
- 1 cup margarine (not butter)
- 4 teaspoon baking powder
- 2 tablespoons anise or vanilla extract

Directions

4. In the bowl of a mixer, beat eggs, adding sugar gradually. Beat until smooth.
5. Add cooled, melted margarine and anise or vanilla extract.
6. Sift flour and baking powder together. Add to egg mixture, stir. The dough will be sticky enough to be dropped by spoon, slightly thicker than a pancake batter.
7. Preheat the pizzelle iron. When hot, place about 1 tablespoon of batter per pizzelle on the iron.
8. Close the lid and cook until pizzelles are a light golden color, about 1 minute.
9. When ready, lift hot pizzelle with a spatula and set on a flat rack to cool. Serve plain or dusted with confectioners' sugar.

Cannoli Pizzelles:
1. While hot, it can be shaped into a cone or rolled into a cylinder. Pizzelles set very quickly, so you may only be able to form a few into cannoli shells.
2. With pastry, tube fill with a cream filling. Filling from each end. (See "Cannoli Ricotta Cream" recipe)

Storage:
Flat and round pizzelles can be stored in an airtight container for up to 1 week. Store cannoli cream filling in the refrigerator in an airtight container for up to 1 week.
Assembled cannoli should be eaten the same day, as the filling will cause the shell to get soggy within 24 hours or less.

Zaletti, Zale

Polenta Cookies

Oven Temp 350°F (180°C)   Bake 12-15 minutes   Yields about 20

Ingredients:

- 1 stick unsalted butter, softened
- ½ cup granulated sugar
- 3 large egg yolks
- ¼ cup milk
- 1 teaspoon baking powder
- ½ teaspoon salt
- Zest of 1 lemon
- 1 teaspoon vanilla extract
- 2 tablespoons marsala wine
- ½ cup raisins
- ¼ cup pine nuts
- 1 cup polenta
- 1½ cup all-purpose flour
- 1 tablespoon granulated sugar
- Confectioners' sugar, for dusting

Directions:

1. Preheat oven to 350°F. Line 2 baking sheets with parchment paper.
2. In the bowl of a mixer, beat sugar and butter until creamy.
3. In a separate bowl, beat egg yolks till fluffy. Add to mixture.
4. Mix in milk, baking powder, salt, lemon zest, vanilla extract, and marsala till blended well.
5. Add raisins and pine nuts. Mix using a spatula or wooden spoon.
6. Slowly add sifted polenta and then flour, alternating each in sections. Mix with a spatula or wooden spoon; you can mix with your hands also till well combined.
7. Roll a tablespoon of dough into a ball and flatten onto a prepared baking sheet. Repeat using all dough.   Leaving about 1 inch in between.
8. Bake about 12-15 minutes till the tops of cookies dry up and the color darkens.
9. Place sheet on rack, allow to cool briefly before removing cookies to rack.
10. When almost cool, sift confectioners' sugar on top. Cool completely.

Esse

Polenta S-shaped Cookies

Oven Temp 350°F (180°C)   Bake 15-18 minutes   Yields about 30

Ingredients:

- 1¾ cups all-purpose flour
- 1 cup Italian polenta or yellow cornmeal
- ½ teaspoon salt
- 1 cup unsalted butter, softened
- ⅔ cup granulated sugar
- Zest of 1 lemon (about 1 tablespoon)
- 1 large egg, plus 1 large egg yolk
- 1 teaspoon vanilla extract

Directions:

1. Line cookie sheets with parchment.
2. Whisk together flour, polenta, and salt in a medium bowl. Set aside.
3. In a large bowl, add butter, sugar, and lemon zest. Beat on medium-high speed until pale and fluffy, about 2 minutes.
4. Add egg and egg yolk, one at a time, beating after each addition. Mix in vanilla.
5. Gradually add flour mixture and beat until combined.
6. Transfer batter to a pastry bag fitted with a ½ inch star tip.
7. Pipe S shapes about 3-inches long and 1-inch wide, spaced 1½ inches apart, onto prepared baking sheets. Place in freezer for 30 minutes before baking.
8. Preheat oven to 350°F. Bake 15-18 minutes until edges are golden.
9. Carefully lift parchment paper and place on wire racks to cool for about 10 minutes. Remove cookies from parchment, and transfer to racks to cool completely.

Note:
Use real polenta or any dry, grainy, coarse-ground cornmeal. Regular cornmeal from the grocery store is often more finely ground and will give your cookies a slightly different texture.

Storage:
Store in airtight container for up to 1 week.

Biscotti Regina

Queen's Biscuits

Oven Temp 350°F (180°C)   Bake 30 minutes   Yields about 24 - 26

Ingredients:

- 2 cups all-purpose flour
- 1/2 cup granulated sugar
- 4 ounces olive oil, butter or solid shortening
- 3 large eggs, separated
- 2 tablespoons whole milk
- 1 tablespoon honey
- Zest of 1 lemon
- 1/4 teaspoon salt
- 3/4 cup sesame seeds, plus more as needed

Directions:

1. Line baking sheets with parchment paper.
2. In a bowl, combine the flour, sugar, and butter until it resembles coarse sand.
3. Add the egg yolks, milk, honey, zest, and salt. Knead until well-mixed dough forms.
4. Roll the dough into a ball, cover with plastic wrap, and refrigerate for at least one hour.
5. Toast the sesame seeds in a dry skillet until golden to dark golden. Transfer to a plate; set aside.
6. Preheat the oven to 350°F.
7. In a small bowl, using a fork, beat the egg whites with 3 tablespoons of water.
8. Divide the chilled dough into 4 sections. Roll each section into a log about 1 inch wide. Cut the logs into 1 1/2-inch sections. Repeat with the remaining dough.
9. Dip each cookie in the egg whites, then roll in the sesame seeds, covering all sides.
10. Place on prepared baking sheets about 2 inches apart.
11. Bake for about 30 minutes, until golden. Cool completely before serving.

Storage:
These cookies may be stored in an airtight container for up to 4 weeks.

Amaretti di Saronno

Saronno Almond Cookie (Crisp)

Oven Temp 340°F (170°C)   Bake 17-23 minutes   Yields about 14

Ingredients:

- 1¼ cups ground almonds
- Scant 1/2 cup granulated sugar
- 1 large egg white, room temperature
- ½ teaspoon almond or vanilla extract

Directions:

1. Preheat oven to 340°F. Line a large baking sheet with parchment paper.
2. If grinding your own whole almonds: Toast almonds and let cool (see note). In a food processor, add the cooled almonds and sugar. Pulse for 20 seconds until very fine. Add egg white and almond extract. Pulse for 30 seconds until the mixture comes together.
3. If using pre-ground almonds: In a food processor, add the ground almonds, sugar, almond extract, and egg white. Pulse until mixture comes together.
4. Roll the dough into small balls and place them about 1 inch apart on the prepared baking sheet. Sprinkle with granulated sugar if desired.
5. Bake for approximately 17 minutes for lighter cookies or up to 23 minutes for traditional cookies, or until golden. Let cool completely.

Toasting Almonds:
Place almonds in a single layer on a baking sheet. Bake for 10 minutes at 350°F (180°C). Toss at least twice during the baking process. Remove to a clean tray and let cool for 30 minutes before grinding.

Amaretti di Sassello

Sassello Almond Cookies (Chewy)

Oven Temp 350°F (180°C)   Bake 12-15 minutes   Yields about 36 - 48

Ingredients:

Variation #1:
- 20 ounces whole peeled almonds
- 5 ounces bitter apricot kernels
- 1⅔ cup granulated sugar

Variation #2:
- 20 ounces almond flour
- 1 teaspoon almond extract
- 12 ounces confectioners' sugar

Both Variations:
- 5 large egg whites
- 1 pinch salt
- 1 cup confectioners' sugar, for dusting

Directions:

Variation #1:
1. Toast almonds in the oven at 350°F until lightly browned. Remove and cool completely.
2. In a food processor, pulse almonds and apricot kernels until coarsely ground.
3. Add sugar and pulse until very fine.

Variation #2:
1. In the bowl of a mixer, blend almond flour, extract, and confectioners' sugar.

Both Variations:
1. Preheat oven to 350°F.
2. In a separate bowl, beat egg whites with a pinch of salt until entirely white and fluffy.
3. Fold egg whites into almond and sugar mix a couple of tablespoons at a time until you get stiff and silky cookie dough. Only use enough egg whites to get the dough together.
4. Sprinkle work surface with confectioners' sugar.
5. Pinch off pieces of dough and roll into 1-inch pieces balls.
6. Roll in a generous amount of confectioners' sugar to coat.
7. Place each cookie on a baking sheet lined with parchment paper. Decorate with an almond (optional).
8. Bake for 12-15 minutes, just until inside crinkles turn light brown.

Storage:
Store in airtight container for up to 1 week. Can freeze up to 2 months.

Paste Di Mandorla

Sicilian Almond Cookies

Oven Temp 350°F (180°C)   Bake 15 - 20 minutes   Yields about 45

Ingredients:

- 6½ cups almond flour
- 2 cups plus 2 tablespoons granulated sugar
- 6 large egg whites
- 2 teaspoons honey
- 1 teaspoon almond extract
- Confectioners' sugar for dusting
- Whole almonds or candied cherries

Directions:

1. Preheat oven to 350°F. Line 2 baking sheets with parchment paper.
2. In a large bowl, mix almond flour and sugar.
3. In a separate bowl, beat egg whites with a whisk until foamy. Set aside approximately one white.
4. Add remaining egg whites to the flour mixture and mix with a spatula.
5. Add honey and almond extract.
6. Mix the dough with your hands, scooping all the dry ingredients from the bottom of the bowl. The dough should be soft but not too sticky. If the dough feels hard and is not coming together, add the remaining egg white.
7. Clean your hands and dust with confectioners' sugar. Take about a tablespoon of dough and roll it in your palms to form a nice, round cookie shape. Set aside on a work surface or tray dusted with confectioners' sugar. Repeat until all dough is used.
8. Sift confectioners' sugar onto the work surface and roll each cookie in it.
9. Arrange cookies on prepared baking sheets, leaving 1 inch spacing between.
10. Decorate with candied cherries, whole almonds, or simply pinch each cookie with your fingers to form an irregular shape.
11. Bake for 15-20 minutes. After 10 minutes, check cookies; adjust baking time if needed to get light color on top and bottoms.

Storage:
Store in airtight container for up to 2 weeks. Can freeze 2 – 3 months.

Cuccidati, Buccellati

Sicilian Fig Cookies

Oven Temp 350°F (180°C)   Bake 20 minutes   Yields about 30

Ingredients:

Dough:
- 2⅓ cups all-purpose flour
- 2 tablespoons granulated sugar
- 2 teaspoon baking powder
- ½ teaspoon salt
- 8 tablespoons frozen unsalted butter, grated
- 2 large eggs
- 1 teaspoon lemon zest
- 2 tablespoons milk

Filling:
- ¾ cup diced dried figs
- 2 tablespoons rum
- 2 tablespoons fresh orange juice
- ⅓ cup honey
- ½ cup chopped dates
- ¼ cup orange marmalade
- 1 cup toasted almond flour
- ½ teaspoon cinnamon
- ¼ teaspoon cloves
- Zest of 1 lemon and 1 orange
- 1 cup hazelnuts, blanched and toasted

Glaze:
- 1 2/3 cups confectioners' sugar
- Juice of one large orange
- 1 tablespoon Fiori di Sicilia
- Colored sprinkles

Directions

Dough:
1. In a large bowl, combine flour, butter, sugar, baking powder, and salt.
2. Cut in the butter until the mixture resembles small peas.
3. Stir in eggs, lemon zest, and milk. Mix until a smooth dough forms.
4. Pat into a ½-inch-thick slab, wrap, and chill for 2 hours or overnight.

Filling:
1. Place all of the ingredients except the hazelnuts into the bowl of a food processor and process until relatively smooth.
2. Chop hazelnuts. Add to mix, pulse three or four times, and transfer to a bowl. Cover and refrigerate for 1 hour.

Assembly:
1. Preheat oven to 350°F°. Line two baking sheets with parchment.
2. Divide the dough into 6 rectangular pieces. Work with one piece at a time, keeping the rest refrigerated.
3. Roll each rectangle into a 3-x-20-x-⅛-inch strip.
4. Take a scant ½ cup of the filling and roll into a ½-inch diameter log, the same length as the dough. Greased hands make this easier.
5. Place filling log onto the long edge of the dough rectangle. Roll the dough over to enclose the filling. Brush edges with water and pinch closed.
6. Flip seam-side-down. Lightly roll with a rolling pin to flatten slightly.
7. Cut each log into 5, 4-inch-long slices. Transfer cookies to prepared baking sheets.
8. Repeat with remaining dough and filling.
9. Bake 20 minutes, until barely golden. Cool pan on a wire rack briefly. Transfer cookies to a wire rack to finish cooling.

Glaze:
1. In a small bowl, combine the confectioners' sugar and juice until smooth. Add the Fiori di Sicilia and mix until a glaze is formed that flows off a spoon but is not too thin.
2. While the cookies are still warm, dip the tops of each in the glaze, allowing the excess to drip off.
3. Place on cooling racks and sprinkle with colored sprinkles. Allow to dry completely.

Storage:
Can store at room temperature in an airtight container for up to 3 weeks. Can be frozen in layers between wax paper up to 3 months.

Biscotti al Pistacchio

Sicilian Pistachio Cookies

Oven Temp 350°F (180°C)   Bake 15 - 18 minutes   Yields about 48 small

Ingredients:
- 3 cups raw unsalted pistachios (shelled)
- 1 1/3 cup almond flour
- 1 cup granulated sugar
- 3 teaspoons honey
- 1 teaspoon vanilla extract
- 1 lemon, zested
- 2 large egg whites
- 3 teaspoons honey
- 2/3 cup confectioners' sugar

Directions:

1. Preheat to oven to 350°F. Line baking sheets with parchment paper.
2. In a food processor, pulse 2 2/3 cup of pistachios and half of the sugar measure until coarsely ground, but not fully ground.
3. Transfer to a large bowl. Add remaining sugar, almond flour, vanilla extract, and lemon zest. Whisk by hand till combined.
4. Add the egg whites and honey. Mix until the batter holds its shape when pressed together.
5. Sift confectioners' sugar into a medium bowl.
6. Pinch off some of the dough, and roll into tablespoon-sized balls. Drop into confectioners' sugar, coating well.
7. Place on baking sheets; leave 2 inches of space between each cookie.
8. Flatten slightly with the bottom of a glass cup or jar.
9. From the remaining pistachios, press a whole pistachio into each cookie for garnish.
10. Bake 15-18 minutes until fragrant, crackled, and golden brown.

Storage:
Store in an airtight container for up to 2 weeks.

Mandorle a Scaglie

Slivered Almond Cookies

Oven Temp 350°F (180°C)   Bake 12-15 minutes   Yields about 30 - 36

Ingredients:

- 1 pound almond paste
- 3 tablespoons cornstarch
- ¾ cup granulated sugar
- 1 cup confectioners' sugar
- 3 large egg whites (about ½ cup)
- 2 tablespoons almond extract
- 12 ounces slivered almonds

Directions:

1. Place almond paste in a large bowl, and break up to the size of small peas.
2. Add cornstarch and sugars. Mix and blend well.
3. In a separate bowl, beat the egg whites until stiff. Gently fold egg whites into the almond mixture, mixing together.
4. Let dough stand for 15 minutes.

Assembly:
1. Preheat oven to 350°F. Grease 2 cookie sheets or line with parchment paper.
2. Spread slivered almonds onto a clean surface. Make teaspoon-sized cookies and roll in slivered almonds.
3. Bake at 350°F for 12-15 minutes, until light golden brown.

Storage:
Store in airtight container for up to 1 week. Can be frozen for up to 2 months.

Bocconotti

Small Bites

Oven Temp 350°F (180°C) Bake 18-20 minutes Yields about 24

Ingredients:

- 2 cups all-purpose flour
- ½ cup granulated sugar
- 1 teaspoon baking soda
- Pinch of salt
- ¾ cup chilled butter, cubed
- 1 large egg
- 1 teaspoon orange zest
- Confectioners' sugar for dusting
- ¾ cup fig jam, concord grape jam, cherry or pineapple preserves

24 Mini-Tart molds or Mini-Muffin pans (2 inches wide)

Directions:

1. Place flour, sugar, baking powder, and salt in a food processor and pulse for a few seconds to combine.
2. Add chilled cubed butter and pulse, just until you achieve coarse crumbs.
3. In a small bowl, whisk together egg and orange zest. Add egg mixture to the food processor.
4. Blend until half of the dough mixture has come together, then transfer to a work surface. Knead gently by hand until the dough forms a ball.
5. Wrap dough in plastic wrap and chill for 1 hour.

Assembly:
1. Preheat oven to 350°F. Grease 24 mini-tart molds or mini-muffin pans.
2. Break off a tablespoon of dough and form into a ball. Press the ball into the mold and up against the edges. Trim off any excess with your fingers.
3. Repeat until all molds are filled. Fill each tart with about 1 teaspoon jam.
4. Take another tablespoon of dough, form into a ball, and press it between two sheets of cling wrap with the palm of your hands.
5. Place the flattened disks over the jam-filled tartlets and press the dough around the mini-molds' edges to seal. Trim any excess dough.
6. Place the mini-tartlets on a baking sheet. Bake until golden brown, about 18-20 minutes. Cool completely. Dust with confectioners' sugar.

Storage:
Store in airtight container at room temperature for up to 2 days, then refrigerate.

Biscotti di San Valentino

St. Valentine Cookie

Oven Temp 350°F (180°C)   Bake 10-12 minutes   Yields about 36

Ingredients:

- 1¼ cups butter, softened
- 1 cup granulated sugar
- 2 large eggs, room temperature
- 3 cups all-purpose flour
- 1 tablespoon baking cocoa
- ½ teaspoon salt
- ¼ teaspoon ground cinnamon
- ¼ teaspoon ground nutmeg
- ⅛ teaspoon ground cloves
- 2 cups ground almonds
- Raspberry jam
- Confectioners' sugar

2 Cookie cutters: 3-inch Heart shape & 1.5-inch Heart shape

Directions:

1. In a large bowl, cream butter and sugar until light and fluffy.
2. Add eggs, 1 at a time, beating well after each addition.
3. Combine flour, cocoa, salt, cinnamon, nutmeg, and cloves. Gradually add to the batter and mix well. Stir in almonds.
4. Refrigerate for 1 hour or until easy to handle.
5. Preheat oven to 350°F. Have 2-3 ungreased baking sheets ready.
6. On a lightly floured surface, roll out dough to ⅛-inch thickness. Cut with a 3-inch heart-shaped cookie cutter.
7. Cut a 1½-inch heart shape in the center of each cookie. Remove center, can knead all center together; roll out for more cookies.
8. Place cookies and their cut-outs on ungreased baking sheets. Bake for 10-12 minutes, or until the edges are golden brown. Remove to wire racks to cool.
9. Spread ½ teaspoon jam over the bottom of the solid, cooled cookies.
10. Sprinkle cut-outs with confectioners' sugar, then carefully place over jam cookie.

Storage:
Store in an airtight container for 2-3 days. Then refrigerate.

Zuccherini

Sugar Cookies

Oven Temp 400°F (200°C)   Bake 10 minutes   Yields about 36

Ingredients

Dough – 2 flavor variations:
- 3/4 cup shortening
- 3/4 cup granulated sugar
- 3 large eggs
- 1 teaspoon vanilla extract (#1) or lemon extract (#2)
- 3 cups all-purpose flour
- 3 teaspoons baking powder
- 1/8 teaspoon salt

Glaze – Vanilla Variation #1:
- 1/4 cup milk
- 2 tablespoons butter, melted
- 1/2 teaspoon vanilla extract
- 2-1/2 cups confectioners' sugar
- Food coloring and sanding sugar, optional

Glaze – Lemon Variation #2:
- 1 cup confectioners' sugar
- 1 – 2 tablespoons heavy cream or whole milk
- 1/4 teaspoon lemon extract
- Colored sprinkles

Directions

Dough:
1. Preheat oven to 400°F. Line baking sheets with parchment paper or ungreased baking sheets.
2. In a large bowl, cream shortening and sugar until light and fluffy.
3. Beat in eggs, mixing after each one. Add vanilla.
4. Combine flour, baking powder, and salt. Gradually add to the creamed mixture and mix well.
5. Shape dough into 1-1/2-inch balls. Place 1 inch apart on baking sheets.

6. Bake 8-10 minutes or until lightly browned. Remove to wire racks to cool.

Glaze – Variation #1:
1. In a small bowl, combine milk, butter, vanilla, and confectioners' sugar until smooth.
2. Tint with food coloring if desired.
3. Dip tops of cookies in icing, allowing excess to drip off.
4. Sprinkle with sanding sugar if desired.
5. Place on waxed paper and let stand until set.

Glaze – Variation #2:
1. Whisk confectioners' sugar, heavy cream (or milk), and lemon extract until smooth, no lumps remaining.
2. Dip tops of cookies in the glaze. Top with sprinkles. Place on a wire rack over a paper towel to catch any drips. Allow glaze to harden.

Storage:
The dough can be made ahead and frozen for up to 3 months. Wrap in plastic wrap; place in an airtight plastic bag, removing as much air as possible. Defrost frozen dough overnight in the refrigerator, then follow baking instructions.

Already baked cookies can be frozen without the glaze. Freeze in an airtight plastic bag, squeezing out all the air. Defrost on the counter; glaze and sprinkle when at room temperature.

Store glazed cookies in airtight containers for up to a week. Layer with parchment paper, so glaze does not spread.

Gemma, Gocce alla Marmellata

Thumbprint Cookies

Oven Temp 350°F (180°C)   Bake 10 - 12 minutes   Yields about 36 - 48

Ingredients

- 3/4 cup granulated sugar
- 3/4 cup margarine
- 2 large eggs, separated
- 1 teaspoon salt
- 1/2 teaspoon almond extract
- 1/2 teaspoon vanilla extract
- 2 cups all-purpose flour
- 1 – 1-1/2 cups hazelnuts or almonds, finely chopped
- Fruit jam or fruit preserves
- Optional: 8 ounces Nutella, 1 ounce gulf wax

Directions

1. Preheat oven to 350°F. Grease baking sheets or line with parchment paper.
2. In a large bowl, cream together margarine and sugar.
3. Add egg yolks, salt, almond, and vanilla extracts. Beat together.
4. Gradually add flour at medium speed, mixing well.
5. Roll dough into 1-inch balls
6. Beat reserved egg whites slightly.
7. Dip dough balls into egg whites, then roll in chopped nuts.
8. Placed on a greased baking sheet 2 inches apart.
9. Make a deep depression in the center of each cookie with a fingertip.
10. Bake 10–12 minutes until firm to the touch and lightly browned.
11. Immediately remove from cookie sheet to cooling rack.
12. While still warm, fill centers with a small amount of any flavor jam, fruit preserves, or Nutella.
13. Allow to cool completely.

Hint: If using Nutella, place 8 ounces of Nutella and 1 ounce of gulf wax (edible wax) in a microwave bowl; melt together on low heat, or melt in the top of a double-boiler on the stove. The wax will harden the Nutella when cooled.

Storage:
Store up to 3 days in airtight container. Refrigerate up to 1 week. Can freeze up to 2 months.

Bruitti ma Buoni

Ugly but Good

Oven Temp 325°F (165°C)   Bake 25 - 30 minutes   Yields about 12

Ingredients:

- 1½ cups hazelnuts, blanched and toasted
- 9 large egg whites
- 1½ cups granulated sugar
- ½ teaspoon pure vanilla extract
- ¼ teaspoon kosher salt
- 4 ounces (¾ cup) bittersweet chocolate (70% cacao)

Directions:

1. Preheat oven to 300°F. Roast hazelnuts on a baking sheet until fragrant and lightly toasted, 10-12 minutes. Let cool briefly, then rub off skins with a clean kitchen towel. Coarsely chop.
2. In a medium bowl, beat egg whites on medium-low speed until foamy, about 4 minutes. Increase speed to medium-high and gradually add sugar. Beat until meringue is stiff and shiny, 3-5 minutes. Beat in vanilla and salt.
3. Scrape the meringue into a large, heavy-bottomed saucepan. Add chopped hazelnuts. Place over medium heat, stirring constantly. Scrape the bottom of the pan to make sure the meringue does not stick and burn. Cook about 15 minutes or until the mixture is light brown and pulls away from the pan's sides. The mixture should look curdled after 5 minutes of cooking.
4. Increase oven temperature to 325°F. Remove pan from heat and let cool to room temperature. Coarsely chop the chocolate and fold in.
5. Scoop mounds, about 2 tablespoons each, onto a parchment-lined baking sheet, spacing about 1 inch apart.
6. Bake until cookies are crisp on the outside, about 25-30 minutes. Transfer sheet to a wire rack and let cool completely.

Storage:
Cookies can be stored in an airtight container at room temperature for up to one week.

Zuccherati

Wedding Rings

Oven temp 350°F (180°C)   Bake 15-20 minutes   Yields about 18

Ingredients:

- ½ cup granulated sugar
- 1 teaspoon finely grated lemon zest
- 2 cups all-purpose flour
- Generous pinch Kosher salt
- ¼ teaspoon baking powder
- 1 teaspoon anise seeds
- 2 tablespoons olive oil
- 2 large eggs
- 1 cup confectioners' sugar
- 2-3 teaspoons freshly squeezed lemon juice

Directions:

Dough:
1. In a medium-sized mixing bowl, combine granulated sugar and grated lemon zest, pressing against the bowl's sides to release the citrus oils.
2. Add flour, salt, and baking powder.
3. Gently crush anise seeds with mortar and pestle or palms, and add to flour mixture.
4. Make a well in the middle of the mixture and add olive oil and eggs. Mix to form a dough. Do not overmix.
5. Gather dough into a ball and cover it in the bowl with a clean kitchen towel. Let rest for 30 minutes.
6. Preheat oven to 350°F. Line 2 large baking sheets with parchment paper.
7. Lightly flour work surface. Pinch off a walnut-sized piece of dough, roll into a 5-inch rope, and flatten to about 3/4-inch wide. Form into a ring and pinch ends together. Place rings 1 inch apart on prepared baking sheets.
8. Bake cookies 15-20 minutes, or until lightly browned.
9. Remove sheets from the oven, leaving cookies on sheets to cool.

Glaze:
1. As the cookies are cooling, mix together confectioners' sugar and 2 teaspoons of lemon juice.
2. Add more juice to achieve an icing consistency of ribbon-like white glue.
3. As cookies are still warm, dip tops halfway into the icing and put cookies into a large paper bag.
4. When all of the cookies are in the bag, gently shake cookies to distribute the icing more evenly.
5. Remove from bag and let dry on wire racks.

Note:
Don't worry if the cookies harden. They'll be perfect for dunking into coffee or wine.

Storage:
Store in an airtight container for up to 2 weeks.

Matrimonios

Wedding Snowball Cookies

Oven Temp 325°F (165°C)   Bake 15 - 20 minutes   Yields about 45

Ingredients:

- 1 1/2 c salted butter organic
- 4 tsp vanilla extract
- 3/4 cup ground walnuts
- 3/4 cup ground hazelnuts
- 3 cup all-purpose flour
- 3/4 cup confectioners' sugar
- 1/2 cup confectioners' sugar for dusting

Directions:

1. Preheat your oven to 325°F. Line large baking sheets with parchment paper.
2. In a large mixing bowl, cream together the butter and 3/4 cup of the confectioners' sugar until fluffy.
3. Add the vanilla extract and gradually add ground walnuts and hazelnuts. Mix until combined.
4. Start adding in the flour little by little until mixed in.
5. Using a small spoon, form the cookies into rounds, a golf ball's size or smaller. Should have about 45 cookies.
6. Arrange all the cookies on the baking sheet without touching each other.
7. Bake for 20 minutes or until barely golden.
8. Remove from oven; allow to cool for a few minutes before rolling them over the reserved confectioners' sugar.
9. Arrange the cookies on a platter and dust with more confectioners' granulated sugar on top before serving.

Storage:
Store in airtight container for up to 5 days. Can freeze for up to 2 months.

Ciambelle al Vino

Wine Cookies

Oven Temp 350°F (180°C)   Bake 20-25 minutes   Yields about 20

Ingredients:

- ½ cup dry white wine (see note)
- ½ cup granulated sugar
- ⅓ cup canola or corn oil
- ¼ teaspoon salt
- ½ teaspoon baking powder
- 2¼ cups all-purpose flour
- Granulated sugar for coating
- Optional: 1/2 - 1 teaspoon anise seeds, crushed or ground

Directions:

1. Preheat oven to 350°F. Line cookie sheets with parchment paper.
2. In a medium bowl, add wine, oil, sugar, salt, baking powder, and anise seeds. Mix well.
3. Gradually add enough flour, a little at a time, to form a soft dough.
4. Transfer to a lightly floured flat surface and knead lightly approximately 10 times. The dough will be soft. Don't over-work it!
5. Cut off a little dough (about a tablespoon) and roll into a small, chubby rope (about 5-6 inches long). Bring ends together to form a circle, and pinch together.
6. Dip in sugar and place on prepared cookie sheets, about 1 inch apart.
7. Bake for 20-25 minutes, or until golden brown.
8. Transfer cookies from pans to wire racks to cool.

Note:
If you are out of white wine, you can easily substitute a dry red wine.

Storage:
Can be stored for 1 week in an airtight container.

Index

Notes

Made in the USA
Coppell, TX
25 October 2024